Jesus

JESUS

Lucas Grollenberg

The Westminster Press
Philadelphia

Translated by John Bowden from the Dutch *Jezus: weg naar hoopvol samen leven* published by Uitgeverij Bosch & Keuning N.V., Baarn

Eighth printing 1977

© Bosch & Keuning N.V. 1974

English translation © John Bowden 1978

PUBLISHED BY THE WESTMINSTER PRESS®
Philadelphia, Pennsylvania

PRINTED IN THE UNITED STATES OF AMERICA

9 8 7 6 5 4 3 2 1

Library of Congress Cataloging in Publication Data

Grollenberg, Lucas Hendricus, 1916–
    Jesus.

    Translation of Jezus, weg naar hoopvol samen
leven.
    1. Jesus Christ—Person and offices.
BT202.G69813   232   78-13478
ISBN 0-664-24232-4

CONTENTS

	Apology	vii
1	The Quest for Jesus	1
2	History Revisited	8
3	Baptism by John	16
4	The Label 'Prophet'	21
5	The Torah and the End of this World	29
6	Jesus Goes his own Way	38
7	'A New Teaching with Authority!'	45
8	Why he Had to Die	59
9	How 'the Church' Began	71
10	Complications Again	87
11	The Mystery of Jesus	100
12	On Being the Church	117
	Translator's Note	127

Apology

In recent years I have talked about Jesus a good deal, mostly with groups of people who have invited me, and sometimes with young couples at their marriage interviews. My publishers asked me to put down in writing something of what I had said. 'Write about Jesus as you talk about him.' I gladly agreed to their request, because many people indicated that they had found our conversations about Jesus useful.

However, I soon had a great disappointment. Sitting by oneself in a room at a typewriter is not at all the same as talking to other people and making contact with them. Of course, the groups which had invited me asked me first and foremost because of my knowledge of the Bible, because I had access to information about Jesus which they did not have. So in our first encounters, I had the role of teacher. But whenever the figure of Jesus is conjured up in some way, whenever we are as it were confronted with him, we all seem equally wise and equally competent (or equally foolish and equally incompetent). When we came together, we would all give some account of ourselves. Sometimes the conversation lapsed into silence. Someone would read part of the gospels, or we experienced the way in which Jesus could still speak to us as we came together and repeated his actions over bread and wine in a simple eucharist.

Sitting at my typewriter I have missed all that. Moreover, in discussions, it is possible to sketch out historical backgrounds quickly, in rather broad terms, leaving out specific details until people ask about them. This makes it possible to tell a story in a somewhat illogical way. In a conversation, the bits and pieces, the questions and answers, in due course begin to make up a coherent picture. But writing is a different matter. Outlines have to be clearer, because the readers will not be able to ask questions afterwards. And if there are too many details – there can never be too many for historical experts! – then readers may perhaps be put off. Writing imposes a discipline. Still, my publishers did ask me to take as little account as possible of the demands of literary style and to write as I usually talk.

The result of all this is a strange kind of book, a conversational book which is also very personal. I may have surprised or annoyed older people by talking freely and apparently light-heartedly about various aspects of belief and church life which they feel to be sacred and unassailable, beyond all criticism. I would like to assure these people that I too have lived in the world of sacred customs and sacred institutions, of unassailable certainties. I did so for years, and I enjoyed it very much, but I think that I have grown out of it now.

I come from what people described as a good Catholic family, so I was protected against anyone who might have had different views. In 1934 I joined the Dominican order, which again gave me a sheltered life within the Catholic church. I led a cloistered existence. During our theological education we heard virtually nothing about the intensive criticisms of Christianity dating back to the previous century, or about the violent revolutions in the life and thought of the European world. At best, these were described to us, only to be rejected as nonsense, in the triumphant tones of people who know that they have the truth. In 1943 I left the monastery to work outside. Because of the German occupation I came in contact with all kinds of people who disagreed with me. Yet they seemed to be good men. I was often surprised by the unselfishness and the courage of humanists, communists, or whatever else they might call themselves.

In 1946 I was sent to Palestine to do biblical research with the French Dominicans in Jerusalem. We were concerned with historical questions: Who wrote the books of the Bible? In what circumstances? What were they really trying to say? I also spent several summers working on archaeological sites. There we dug in the homes of ancient peoples and discovered their buildings, their artefacts and their skeletons.

After that I spent a number of years introducing young Dominicans to the world of the Bible. I taught them to ask what sort of a man Isaiah was, what the Jews who wrote Deuteronomy or Proverbs had in mind, what they seemed like to people of their own time, and what they wanted to do. After about ten years I was allowed to lecture on the parables in the gospels. Since then my view of Jesus, in other words my view of what he really wanted and how it inevitably brought him into conflict with Jewish society, has steadily become clearer.

I have been increasingly preoccupied with Jesus, and as a result I have gradually become less concerned about all kinds of 'truths' from the past: doctrines of God and the Trinity, of Christ as the God-man, of the means of grace, the infallibility of Christian dogma, biblical inspiration, and so on. It is not that these are no longer true for me; they are no longer relevant, and do not fit in with the rest of my thinking.

As a result, I have grown away from the world of unassailable institutions and divine certainties in which I grew up. This seems to have been my own particular involvement in a development in which everyone has one part or another, whether they like it or not. Many devout Christians find this development difficult and painful, sometimes causing personal dramas which bite deeply into their lives. As things have turned out, I am still a member of the Dominican order, and can live and work within a loving brotherhood, among colleagues who are trying to embody the spirit of Jesus. I count that a great privilege.

1

The Quest for Jesus

Jesus must have been a good man. Everyone is agreed on that. He preached love, and he showed it to everyone whom he met. He was amazingly good. So why was he put to death in the cruellest way imaginable?

Jesus died a most shameful death. He was nailed hand and foot to a cross, so that he could move only his head. You can see what it was like from the film of *Jesus Christ Superstar*.

And that was only the beginning. Crucifixion dragged on for a terribly long time, hour after hour, with appalling pain, cramp and thirst. It was the punishment for disobedient slaves and trouble-makers. Which makes us ask again, Why did Jesus suffer such a punishment if he was as good as all that?

What happened after Jesus' terrible death is even stranger. Some of his friends claimed that he had appeared among them again, just as he had been. There he was, all of a sudden – and such appearances happened more than once. Because of this they began to see the horrific end to his life as the beginning of a new time. They could sense this new time themselves, because they had become new men, with new hopes and new expectations. Moreover, what had happened to them seemed to be catching. They felt that they had to pass their experiences on to others, and when these others heard the story, they too were captivated by it. They too found a new way of looking at themselves and the world around, and they too were seized by a new hope.

The story of Jesus evidently did more than simply impart information. When people listened to it, they did not just say politely, 'That's an interesting tale!' It obviously had the same quality as a good film or play, the kind that affects us deeply and continues to leave its mark on us for hours or even days afterwards. And in fact the story of Jesus seems to have had even more of a profound influence than that, since it changed men's lives. We know how meeting someone can change our whole life and give it a totally new direction. Jesus made the same kind of impact when people heard his story and came under its spell. Yet how could that be, seeing that he was dead and buried?

In those first days there was no doubting the effect Jesus had. Twenty years after the crucifixion of Jesus his story was already being told in the great cities of the eastern Mediterranean. It spread like a forest fire and people everywhere got caught up in it. They formed groups, and became a kind of Jesus movement. They met together regularly, and claimed that they were commemorating his death. It might seem strange that anyone could keep going back to something as grisly as a death by crucifixion. Yet that is what these people did as they met together, drawn from all walks of life, educated and uneducated alike. They said that the crucified Jew in distant Palestine had totally transformed and renewed their lives. But again, how could that be?

You might well wonder how this Jesus could have deluded his followers into thinking that his failure on the cross was really some kind of victory over the powers of this world. You might press your question even harder once you realized that his followers had known him for only a short time. Scholars are certain that Jesus' ministry lasted at most three years, and probably even less. The founders of other religions had much more of an opportunity to make disciples. Buddha was in his thirties when he experienced his great 'enlightenment'. After that he travelled all round the northern parts of India, proclaiming his teaching and his new way to redemption. He was eighty years old when he died, in about 480 BC. So he had more than forty years in which to pass on his teaching. Mohammed was not quite so fortunate. He received his first 'revelations' when he was forty, but after that he still had twenty-two years in which to spread his belief in Allah. He died of a sudden illness in the year 632 of our era.

Furthermore, Jesus did not die either of old age or of sickness,

2

nor was he surrounded by great crowds of wondering disciples. After a year or two of itinerant preaching he was put to death as a criminal, despised and even hated. His few followers had abandoned him to his fate. Shortly afterwards, the same followers claimed that he was among them again, quite differently from before, but in a way which they felt to be much more real. It was this very belief in the crucified Jesus who was still alive that spread with such incredible speed. Someone in a Jesus-group in a city on the Mediterranean coast might suddenly begin to speak in the name of Jesus. And the cry would be heard: 'See, I was dead and yet I am alive!'

How did Jesus manage all this in such a short time? That is the next question. Of course, there is an old answer to it, which you can hear in churches and in Sunday schools. This answer is taken for granted, though in fact it is not really an answer, because there is no questioning to go with it. Many church people would be horrified if someone were to ask, 'How did Jesus manage all this?' They would feel that such a question was irreverent and superfluous; it was wrong and unnecessary because what we see in Jesus is God's work. Jesus is the Son of God. Before God made the world, Jesus was with the Father in heaven. At a time decreed by God, the Son came down from heaven to earth and lived a human life among us. Jesus Christ is God and man in one person. The Father had decreed that his Son should suffer and die in order to atone for men's sins. Through his cross he has brought redemption for every one of us. After his death he rose from the grave, appeared to his followers, the disciples, and then ascended into heaven. He now sits there at the right hand of the Father and sends down his Spirit upon us. This Holy Spirit moves a man's heart to seek his salvation in the cross of Christ, and faith provides the way to eternal life, to happiness after death.

Many believers still talk about Jesus in this way, in words which they learned at Sunday school. And they still use the same vocabulary Sunday by Sunday when in hymns and prayers they express the faith which gives them security and peace of mind. Our question, 'How did Jesus manage it all?', must inevitably sound irreverent to these people, because it is the question of an outsider. To a believer it goes without saying that everything that Jesus brought about, including the movement which arose after his death, was and is unique and incomparable. It was all God's work. God himself came among us in the person of Jesus.

For most of us, however, this way of talking has become incomprehensible. That is why fewer people go to church nowadays. 'That kind of language doesn't make sense any more', they say. 'The word "God" keeps coming up all the time and we don't know what to make of it.' Perhaps it once suggested a figure high up above us, in heaven, an omnipotent Being who made the universe and sees whatever happens on earth, who holds everything in his hand and has it under his control. Perhaps children still think in this way, but they will be the very little ones. Even primary schools often have on classroom walls a beautiful colour poster of our earth made from a photograph which the Americans took on the moon. Against a jet-black background you can see a bluish sphere on which it is possible to distinguish parts of the continents and the oceans, and banks of cloud. The photograph was taken from a long way up and a long way away. Beyond that, and even farther away, is endless space with its stars and solar systems, from which light and radiation come to our earth. God is not to be found anywhere in space, nor is heaven.

Yes, believers say, but we don't really look for God there. He isn't anywhere in the universe. He is invisible, the power which is present everywhere, guiding and governing all things. He is the one about whom we sing so often in the psalms: 'He is king over the whole earth and he governs the people righteously.' But he is invisible, so it is impossible to prove that he exists. That is a matter of faith.

But can we really believe in the existence of such a power which is involved in all that happens and must be righteous and good in all its dealings? We don't see any evidence of it: quite the opposite. Anyone will be able to give examples of what I mean. I think first of my neighbour's wife, dying of a blood disease at the age of twenty-nine, to the despair of her husband. Her two small children still know nothing. She is a dear, fine

4

woman. Is that fair? And many other people come to mind, an ever-widening circle. Then on the horizon are the millions of people who die of hunger and undernourishment, while we live in prosperity. Is that a just ordering of the world? There are some words which people sing in church that I simply cannot bring myself to join in:

> Great are the works of the Lord,
> studied by all who have pleasure in them,
> Full of honour and majesty is his work,
> and his righteousness endures for ever.

They come from an old Jewish psalm. But even Jews find it difficult to sing them, despite the almost innate Jewish belief in God's rule of the world. In this connection, I am thinking of a book by the American rabbi Richard Rubenstein. *After Auschwitz*, which was published in 1966. Rubenstein has no doubt at all that after the murder of six million Jews, the two main beliefs of Judaism are no longer tenable, namely that there is a God who directs history and that this God has a special concern for the Jewish people. If these beliefs were true, Rubenstein writes, then God would have known in advance about this mass murder and would have incorporated it into his plan. 'I would rather live in an absurd, irrational universe than believe that.'

God did not intervene in Auschwitz. And that reminds me of another Jew who lost his faith in God long before the mass-murders, in the Polish city of Chrzanow, not far from Auschwitz. His name was Isaac Deutscher, and he has given a personal description of how it happened, in 1921, when he was fourteen years old. His father wanted to live as an orthodox Jew and at the same time to be a man of the modern world. He wrestled with this problem and often talked about it with Isaac. So the young boy began to doubt from a very early stage. He had a friend, an apprentice at their printing works, who challenged him to prove whether or not God existed. They chose the Day of Atonement as the time of the test. Pious Jews fast for the whole of that day, and do not even drink any water. While the faithful were all in the synagogue, Isaac had to go to the cemetery, where his friend was waiting for him. There Isaac took two ham sandwiches out of his bag. Eating these contravened two rules contained in the Law: it was strictly forbidden for Jews to eat the meat of pigs, or to mix meat and milk products like butter. Isaac was to commit a number of deadly sins, eating strictly forbidden food, on the Day of Atonement, in a cemetery and at the grave of a rabbi, to prove that he no longer believed in God. Later he described how he felt when he was tasting the forbidden food. 'I half-hoped and half-feared that something terrible would happen; I waited for a thunder that would strike me down. But nothing happened.' God did not intervene in Chrzanow, any more than he intervened in Auschwitz. Now a God who does nothing does not exist; so from that moment on, Isaac became a convinced atheist.

A great many people think as he did. No one can believe in a God who holds all the strings in his hands and every now and then 'intervenes' decisively in our human world. Such a God does not exist. But if that is the case, he did not exist in the time of Jesus either. So he cannot be introduced to explain the phenomenon of Jesus.

However, that is what people try to do, if only because they are human and look for explanations of things which at first sight seem inexplicable. In this case they try to explain the figure of an ordinary Jew who set a world-wide movement in motion after no more than a year or two. How did he manage it? There is also a desire to know because the figure of Jesus has caught the imagination of so many people in recent years. The film of *Jesus Christ Superstar* has run for months in every town, and the songs from it can still be heard everywhere. Young people meet together in a great variety of Jesus groups. Furthermore, in the last few years more books have been published about Jesus than at any other time in history. They keep appearing in an ever-growing flood. There are novels, and bestsellers with a scholarly flavour to them. There are also learned books, which are not only written by biblical scholars and theologians, or by churchmen. Psychologists have been involved in a series of studies on Jesus and Freud, and the Czech philosopher, Milan Machoveč, a convinced Marxist, has

6

written a thoughtful book about him. Machoveč has great admiration for Jesus and wrote his resolute testimony to the future of mankind under the title *A Marxist Looks at Jesus*.

The reason for this interest seems to be that people with very different views can see something in Jesus; they have a vague feeling that he has something to do with the meaning and purpose of our lives, and has something to say about the countless questions which confront us. However, it is easy to be perplexed by the flood of films and books, and by the accumulation of portraits, fantasies, claims and feelings about Jesus. If you want to form your own opinion you have to go back in history almost two thousand years. You need to investigate the facts about Jesus, how he will have lived and thought in the world of his time, what he did and said, and why it cost him his life; and what kind of people became his followers after his death. That will provide an objective basis, something that can be discussed. Then it will be possible to work out what the facts might mean for us today, and how they might help us to work out a pattern for living together.

— 2 —

History Revisited

If we want to know anything about Jesus, or the impression he made on the people whom he met, we have to use our imagination. We have to think ourselves back into the society of first-century Palestine. But is that possible? Can we transplant ourselves into the life of people who lived so long ago and so far away? Anyone who comes from Groningen, in North Holland, will feel that the people of Limburg are very different. They speak with a lilt, and use a soft g, and at carnival time there is no one to touch them. They celebrate their festival in an inimitable way, which leaves everyone else standing. Further south, in France or Spain, people will seem even stranger, and even more difficult to understand, while on the other side of the Mediterranean, in North Africa, the world is utterly different, if not incomprehensible. Women walk down the street so wrapped up in veils that you can only see their eyes, and men kiss one another. A friend who has lived there for twenty years and has learnt the language says that he still feels a foreigner.

Add to this a gap of two thousand years, and it seems quite impossible to enter into the life, the feelings, the thought and the habits of the Palestinian Jews, from among whom Jesus came.

Still, we have to make the attempt. This is not as hopeless as it might seem. We know a good deal about Jewish society in Palestine in the time of Jesus. It would be wrong to think that the country was under-developed and primitive; it had many contacts with the outside world. In fact, Palestine was by no means inferior to other centres of culture in the Roman empire. It, too, was a land where people read and studied a good deal,

8

in a variety of languages. They were interested in history and geography, in religion and in all the deeper questions of life. Most of the Jews lived a long way from Palestine, in almost all the great cities of the empire. But they looked upon Jerusalem as their religious capital. Their faith formed a bond between them, and that faith included a love of the Temple, 'the house' of their God in Jerusalem. They supported it year by year with payments of money, and those who could afford to visit the holy city went at least once in their life, or even several times.

Not only Jews, but also Roman and Greek writers wrote books about Palestinian society and culture. Many of their works have survived. In addition, we have all kinds of other relics of Palestinian society: letters, bills, coins, inscriptions, the remains of buildings and even of substantial parts of cities. Since the beginning of the last century scholars have tried to fit together all the facts about Palestinian society to provide a picture of everyday life there. They have written vast books about it. I have a whole series of them in my study. If you looked at all the books about Palestine, you might well think that we now know all there is to know. But that is not the case. Books still continue to appear, because new facts keep emerging, and people of our day keep considering them from new perspectives.

There are new facts. As an example let me mention something that everyone knows about: the Dead Sea Scrolls. They were discovered in 1947. We had known for a long while, from the old history books of the Romans, the Greeks and the Jews, that at the time of Jesus the parties within Judaism included a group called the Essenes. We also had some information about the way in which these people lived and thought, but it was all rather vague. Then the scrolls were found, in caves and holes on the steep mountain slopes which drop down to the Dead Sea. They seem to have been a sort of Essene library. At the foot of the mountain face was an enormous pile of debris, a hill of rubble, of the kind that exists by the hundred all over the Middle East. Whenever archaeologists come across such hills, they examine the fragments of pottery that can always be found in them and use these to determine the date of the ruins. This particular pile of debris by the Dead Sea had been thought to be

9

Roman, the remains of one of a series of fortified outposts. However, when the scrolls were found, along with thousands of fragments, the remains of all kinds of writings, archaeologists began to investigate it more closely. In their excavating work they did not discover a Roman outpost, but the chief building of the Essene community, a kind of monastery.

I have been on the site myself, and I much enjoy talking about my experiences there. It was at the end of March 1953, when the excavators were carefully removing sand and rubble from an area between four walls which at that stage were only about three feet high. Strangely shaped fragments of plaster began to appear from the sand, and we wondered what they might be. Were they some kind of decoration from the ceiling? When everything had been taken out and we began to fit the fragments together, they seemed to form an enormous long table. We also found a few inkpots. We concluded that we had found the Essene *scriptorium*, the place where they had so devotedly copied the books of the Bible and other writings which they thought to be important. It was a tremendous experience, to stand in the place where those pious Jews who called their group 'the elect of the new covenant' had sat writing, looking forward to the kingdom of God, while elsewhere in the country Jesus was travelling around preaching on the basis of the same kind of hope.

All this means that we have new facts about a group of Jesus' fellow-countrymen, their beliefs and their expectations, their way of life and their history. This small episode has shed a new light on the whole of Jewish society. It has given rise to a new series of studies about the Essenes as a part of that society. The discoveries also shed more light on Jesus and the groups which came into being after his time. We can now see not only similarities between Jesus and the Essenes, but also the distinctive features of the Jesus movement. And who knows how many other such discoveries may be just around the corner?

We keep making new discoveries of this sort about the past, and at the same time contemporary scholars can begin to look at the ancient world in a new way. One might say that they do not look at it from the same perspective as their predecessors.

For example, in our day, we have become more aware of the way in which economic and social conditions can influence all kinds of developments, including movements which were once supposed to be purely intellectual or spiritual. Scholars always wear the spectacles of their own times, and when they look through them at the ancient world they always have a different view from that of the scholars of an earlier period. Psychology, too, has tinted these spectacles and affected the way in which we look at the past. The result is that our understanding and assessment of the great personalities of history may prove to be rather different.

The four gospels, in which Jesus appears as the leading figure, also come from ancient times. They are documents from the first century, and contain almost everything that was remembered about Jesus. If you were to take them out of the Bible and treat them by themselves, they would not seem to amount to much more than four thin pamphlets. All four together could easily be printed in a Sunday paper without using any special type. I cannot think of any other literature which is so brief and yet has occupied so many scholars for such a length of time. Hundreds of them are still busily at work on it, spread over all the great universities of the world. They keep in touch with one another through learned journals and conferences. If one of them has discovered a new way of interpreting a passage from a gospel, he has his finding published, thus submitting it to the judgment of his colleagues. They look at it, discuss its strong points and its weak points, and incorporate any lessons they may have learnt from it in their own considerations. In this way, more and more light is shed on the extremely complicated history of these four deceptively simple books.

It is now generally accepted that about a generation elapsed between the death of Jesus and the writing of the gospels. The gospels are not factual accounts of what Jesus said and did and of what happened to him; rather, they reflect the views of people living almost half a century later. So there is a long development between the impression which Jesus made and the experiences of his closest friends, and the stories and accounts

11

which were presented by the four gospels. As I have just pointed out, the investigation into this development is in full swing and it will continue for the same reason that historical study is bound to continue: new facts are constantly discovered, and as a result some of our views keep changing. Over recent years, however, a number of conclusions have been reached on which there can be no going back. Above all, thanks to the work of scholars, we know enough to be able to sketch out what Jesus really intended, where he planned to work, how he announced his intentions and what brought him into conflict with the leaders of Jewish society in the Palestine of his time. We now also know a great deal about the people on whom the story of Jesus made such an enormous impact in the earliest days.

We shall now look at the historical evidence, but we shall never come across a God who 'intervenes'. We shall hear a lot *about* him, because the people with whom we shall be concerned spoke about him a great deal. They claimed to be able to do (and to help others to do) all kinds of things, and cherished all kinds of expectations, because of the God in whom they professed a belief, so at least we can try to see how far we feel that they became more or less human as a result of that belief.

Perhaps it is worth developing this thought in rather more detail. We could, of course, stress on the one hand that people in other lands and other cultures seem strange to us, that it is difficult to feel at home with them, difficult to become identified with their concerns and their preoccupations. And of course it is always even more difficult when these people lived two thousand years ago. On the other hand, historical research may make it possible for us to get a bit nearer to the past; and in any case, are not the differences in language and culture, in thought and feeling, really only superficial? Or to put it another way, do not all human beings have a close affinity when it comes to deeper feelings and experiences?

Let me remind you of a well-known illustration. A solitary traveller is ambushed. The robbers almost kill him, rob him of his money, and leave him lying somewhere down the road. He is badly wounded and in agonizing pain; he cannot move and can scarcely utter a sound. He lies there hoping against hope that help will come. And at last someone does come. This traveller sees the wounded man lying there, but does nothing about him, and goes on his way. The unfortunate victim feels angry, hurt, wretched and desperate. It is agony to be left all alone in such a miserable plight. Then another traveller comes along. The victim's hopes begin to revive. Perhaps this man will . . . But the second traveller also does nothing, and goes on his way. The victim now feels even worse than he did before. Then a man comes along with a horse and cart. He stops, gets down, inspects the wounded man and then puts him carefully into the cart. He says nothing; he simply gets on with what needs to be done. He binds up the wounds, and takes the victim to a good hotel. He has to continue with his journey, but promises to come back soon and pay the bill.

The feelings of the wounded man have now changed completely. From the moment when his rescuer stopped and bent over him he felt new life and boundless gratitude welling up in him. Wouldn't things be the same in any culture, at any time? Does not any human being, of whatever time or place, recognize this? Loneliness and desperation on the one hand, and on the other the response that springs up towards someone who helps: new hope, new prospects, gratitude?

To be human means to be dependent on other people. That happens from the time we are born. Unless we are helped at that stage, we die. And we become 'someone' only in our relationship to others. When we emerge from our first close ties, and leave our parents and family, we may fall in love. Something 'comes over' us; that's the way we feel. Whenever we love someone else deeply, with our whole being, and the other person loves us, we feel that we have found and been given something. The experience is overwhelming. We feel inexpressibly happy. Love makes everything seem new. Everything turns out well. Here too we feel that to be truly human we are directed towards other people.

However, we are all familiar with a very different kind of experience, no matter where in the world we may live. Once we have some good fortune, we want to hang on to it. We want to make sure of it, because we feel that it is threatened. As indeed it is, no matter who we are. I need only mention the most terrible threat of all. We all die. Plants and animals also die, but what distinguishes us from other organisms is our awareness of death. Death is really the only certain point in anyone's future: some time, sooner or later, we shall no longer exist.

No one likes thinking about death very much. Perhaps the fear of death is one of the driving forces behind most of what we do. Perhaps we strive to get as much as possible and hold on to it tightly in order to give ourselves a form of security.

Be this as it may, we were considering whether there is an affinity between people from a wide variety of times and places and whether they share each others' feelings in the most profound situations of human life, in the search for friendship and love and the struggle against the inevitability of death. Because Jesus spoke to the people of his time on this deeper level, we can understand why he can still speak to us today. Perhaps this is one way of understanding the real reason why words like 'God' and 'divine' came to be used of him, since these are words which from time immemorial have been used for the secret depths within us, the source of our being, the wellspring of our life.

However, as we look at the details of the story of Jesus we shall not be using these terms. Some people may perhaps find this strange. Many Christians are so familiar with expressions like 'the Godhead of Christ' and the 'God-man' that they imagine Jesus as someone who is both man and God, a kind of dual personality. This idea seems to lie behind the question that one often hears: 'What would Jesus look like if he were to come to earth today?' Those who ask it seem to be thinking of someone existing outside our world, with definite ideas and plans, who then chooses a moment at which to join us in our history.

But that is impossible. There are certain things which human beings cannot choose. We cannot choose our parents. We begin to exist in a particular country, with a particular language, in a particular district, against a particular social background with certain accepted patterns of living and thinking. It is never possible to choose these things. Some choices can be

14

made, but they come later. We cannot choose our mother tongue, but later we can learn another language. We did not choose our original social background; but later we may change it. To begin with, our thought may be influenced by our parents or our environment, but later we can begin to think in our own way. The kind of person we become, our identity, is determined by the choices we make, in important matters or in unimportant ones, in those which affect only ourselves and our own small circle, or in those that have consequences for countless fellow human beings. This process of choosing goes on until we die. After that, as it were, we enter into history, or rather, we belong to the past. We are incapable of further change; we are the people we have become as a result of the choices we have made throughout our lives, in constantly varying circumstances.

This is why an ancient lawgiver (I think it was Solon of Athens) once said: 'You cannot really judge anyone until he is dead.' He was probably thinking of the surprising and unexpected way in which anyone may suddenly begin to think or act in a different way.

In any case, had Jesus lived at another time and in another place, he would not have been Jesus, but someone else. If we are to get to know him, we must also get to know as thoroughly as possible the world in which he lived and the choices that were open to him. The choices shaped the Jesus who went down in history as a man who can have meaning for us. Of course it was Jesus who reminded me of the saying of Solon (or whoever it was). I saw a connection between it and the fact that Christians have always commemorated Jesus' death, right from the beginning. Jesus' death is what made him the 'complete' person who entered history, and it was all the more significant because it was the result of his own choice.

To begin to understand something of the world in which Jesus lived, Jewish society in Palestine, we need to know its history. Moreover, people and events from their past were very real to the Jews. But I would rather not begin with this earlier history. I would prefer to mention it only where it is needed to explain the choices that Jesus made. So I shall begin with the first choice in which we know him to have been involved.

— 3 —

Baptism by John

In the wilderness along the banks of the Jordan a certain John began to announce that the last judgment was imminent. News of this came to Nazareth, and seems to have caused a man called Jesus to drop everything in order to visit him. The whole situation is difficult for us to take in all at once: someone who gave people the fright of their lives with a forecast which came to nothing, and a Jesus who believed in him. Moreover, this visit to the Jordan is the first historical information that we have about Jesus. Scholars are quite sure about that. We do not know anything about his earlier life. His father was called Joseph and his mother Mary, and the first Christians also knew that he had brothers and sisters. The brothers were called Jacob, Joses, Judas and Simon, which were all Jewish names in that part of Palestine. Parents quite often called their sons Jesus; it was the Greek form of Joshua, or Yehoshua, as it was pronounced by the majority of Jews.

That is almost all the information we have: the place Nazareth and a few names, including those of Jesus' parents and brothers. Joseph was a carpenter and Jesus also seems to have worked at the same trade. It is a pity that we do not know more, because early family background has a great influence on a person's later life. That is why we should very much like to have more information about Joseph and Mary and their families. What sort of people were they, and what was their social status? Did Jesus go to school in Nazareth? What sort of school was it? In the Palestine of Jesus' time, and certainly in the northern area of Galilee in which Nazareth was situated, the Jews had many different life-styles, and very different standpoints and expecta-

16

tions, in both religion and politics. We just do not know where Jesus' family stood in all this.

This gap in our knowledge about Jesus' first years was filled in later by Christians. Almost everyone in our Western world knows the stories about the miraculous beginning to Jesus' life, how an angel came to Mary to tell her that she was pregnant without having had relations with a man, and how angels announced to shepherds in the fields that Jesus was born in Bethlehem. Then there were the wise men (to become the three kings in later stories) who came from the East to pay homage to the newborn Jesus. An angel also intervened to give a warning which enabled him to escape the wrath of king Herod, who had all the babies in Bethlehem and the surrounding district put to death. When Jesus was twelve years old, he is said to have astounded the scholars in the Temple in Jerusalem by his insight into religious matters. But these stories are not exactly reminiscences of what happened; they do not give us any historical information about Jesus' birth and his boyhood.

So he really comes into view only when he goes to John by the Jordan, and has himself baptized there. The first Christians remembered that his baptism was of decisive importance for Jesus. They expressed this by putting the event as it were in a miraculous setting. They described how at that moment Jesus had a kind of vision: the heavens opened before him, the Holy Spirit descended on him in the form of a dove, and he heard a voice say, 'You are my beloved Son, in you I am well pleased.' They also remembered how Jesus spoke about John the Baptist with great admiration: 'Among those born of women, no greater has appeared than John the Baptist.' The remark may sound somewhat exaggerated, but Jesus often spoke in an exaggerated way. We shall discover that in due course, and with luck we shall get used to it, once we begin to understand what he was getting at. In any event, remarks like this indicate that Jesus had a very high opinion of John. Some Christians even recalled that he worked alongside John for some time and helped him to baptize the people who listened to John's summons and were ready to undergo John's baptism as a sign of their conversion.

17

Because John was obviously so important to Jesus, we must look at him rather more closely. What was the aim of this remarkable man and why did he baptize, as a sign of conversion and repentance? Christians remembered that John had been possessed by a single thought, or rather by an event which he expected soon, in the very near future. This event was the end of all wickedness and all evil, in a devastating divine judgment. John was utterly convinced that it was imminent, and he proclaimed the fact in imagery which the people of his time could not easily forget. 'The axe is laid to the root of the tree.' We say that a barren fruit tree needs to be cut down, without thinking twice about it. But every Jew was also familiar with the way in which the symbol of a tree and its fruits can be applied to people. Someone who is upright and honourable and cares for others as God wills, is a fruitful tree and brings forth good fruit. Anyone who does evil, in whatever way, is a tree with bad fruit. The symbol can also be applied to a group or even to a whole people. All Jews had more or less vivid expectations that one day God would come to judge. Then, to use this imagery, he would cut down the barren trees. The Jews thought that this would happen one day in the future, but John announced, almost shouted: 'Look, it's going to happen now; the axe is laid at the root of the tree!'

John also used another image, which was very evocative for people in Palestine, where corn was grown in so many places. When the corn was ripe, it was cut and brought to the threshing floor. There it was put in a heap and threshed, rolled and chopped in order to strip the grains of corn from the ears. After that a basket or sieve was used to separate the precious grain from the straw and the chaff. This was known as a winnowing fan. This image was also applied in the Bible to the judgment that God would accomplish, distinguishing the good men from the bad, separating the corn from the chaff. In order to indicate that God's judgment was imminent, inexorably close, John announced, 'He already has his fan in his hand.' The judge is not like a farmer standing and thinking, 'Sometime I ought to go down to the threshing floor.' No, he has his fan in his hand and will start any moment now.

The words of John which Christians remembered do not make it clear what form God's judgment was going to take. God might appear in person but the judge might also be a superhuman figure. This figure would be so immeasurably greater and more powerful than John himself, that John felt no more than a slave in comparison. 'I am not even worthy to undo his shoes.'

According to John, the only chance, the only way of surviving the coming judgment was to be baptized, dipped in the water of the river Jordan. Or, to put it more accurately, the only chance was to change one's life-style completely, in the way symbolized by baptism. Baptism was a token that a man's whole life had been submitted to the will of God. That, and nothing else, was the basis for his righteousness. In times long past, God's people had come into being through the waters of the Red Sea by escaping from slavery in Egypt. A new generation of Israelites had come into the Promised Land through the water of the Jordan. So those who had undergone John's baptism would be able to stand firm at God's judgment, unaffected by the impending inferno which would consume all those who did not repent, because this baptism showed the seriousness of their concern to be right with God. Fire, too, was an old biblical image for God's judgment. John said that barren trees would be thrown into the fire, and that the chaff would be burnt in it also. He baptized with water, but the one whom he proclaimed would baptize with fire.

John the Baptist addressed his summons to all Jews without exception. It was certainly not his intention to make those who had been baptized into a group apart, a kind of church community or sect. There was no time for that. Above all, he summoned 'all Israel' to repentance. Later, after his death, his followers do seem to have banded together. But while he was alive, those who had been baptized probably returned to their own villages, to their families and their work. They may have felt rather isolated and different from their neighbours, intent as they were on the impending judgment, full of tense expectation, while others went on living their ordinary everyday life.

Jesus, too, will have been one of these isolated figures. Regardless of whether or not he worked with John for some length of time, he will also have been eager and expectant, full of the impending judgment and the repentance which it demanded.

We may be certain that Jesus was influenced by the strange figure of John. John's appearance and way of life were also out of the ordinary. He wore a coat of coarse camel hair with a leather belt round his waist, and he fed on what he could find in the wilderness along the bank of the Jordan, locusts and wild honey. The greatest problem that he presents is, of course, that his forecast never came true. The judgment did not take place. The world followed its usual course and evil men were not destroyed by fire. What does that indicate? We ought to think about this for a while, especially as we shall find that Jesus, too, expected an imminent judgment.

— 4 —

The Label 'Prophet'

John the Baptist was quite exceptional, even to the Jews of his time. Perhaps many people came to see him out of curiosity. Anyone who had to travel to the area on the other side of the Jordan would have to go through the strip of wilderness along the river bank, so a visit to John would not have been much of a detour. On arrival, they would find themselves among the other onlookers, and would have heard the lean man in his coat of hair proclaiming that judgment was near and that everyone had to repent. 'Do not say, "I am a good Jew, a son of Abraham, beloved of God, and the judgment will not affect me." No, you are all vile and wicked, poisonous snakes, adders. You have no chance in the coming judgment. If God wants a people for himself, he will have to create a new Israel. He can do that easily enough! He can make as many sons of Abraham as he wants out of these dead stones here.' In Aramaic, the language which the Jews of the time used in speaking to one another, the word for 'stone' and the word for 'son' were almost indistinguishable. It is difficult to put John's word-play into English, but what he meant is clear enough: no one can rely on being a Jew to survive this judgment. Everything depends on how you have acted as a human being.

John was not only eccentric, but also rather presumptuous. He was evidently convinced of his unique mission. People had to be baptized by him if they were to have any future. It sounds rather pretentious for someone to suppose that the future of others is bound up with him and depends on him. Jesus taught on similar lines to John, and we shall find the same characteristic in him: perhaps Jesus had an even stronger sense of a special

21

divine mission.

Although John was quite exceptional, even for the Jews of his time, they could place him fairly easily. They had a label for him. Suppose you are sitting with a close friend and someone comes in wearing odd clothes and uttering all kinds of strange sounds. You may be quite horrified, until someone gives him a label. 'O, he's an artist!' Or, 'He comes from the mental hospital down the road.' Then you will recover from the first shock; you will have placed the person, given him a label. In the same way, the Jews could give John a label: he was a prophet.

What did this word mean to the Jews of the time, including Jesus himself? Jesus called John a prophet, and indeed more than a prophet, and we shall see that he also spoke of himself in the same way.

We tend to think of a prophet as someone who foretells the future. He knows what will happen in the immediate future, or even much later on. For example, it is possible to forecast the weather for next weekend. On that basis people may plan to go somewhere, and it is annoying when their plans do not work out. At Christmas we hear how prophets had announced the birth of Christ centuries earlier. Their forecasts turned out right. This shows that Christ really did come from God, because God is the only one who knows the future. So he had 'revealed' to the ancient prophets what he was going to do in Bethlehem later. The prophets also forecast the course of Christ's life, his death and resurrection. And, people say, 'We really cannot understand why the Jews did not accept him, especially since it was all put so clearly in the scriptures . . .'

However, it does not seem to be so clear when we read the scriptures by ourselves. It is by no means simple. We need a good deal of effort and patience to form a picture of the great figures of the prophets, Amos, Hosea, Isaiah, Micah, Jeremiah and Ezekiel, from the confusion of texts. I have mentioned the greatest of them here in historical order, and not in the biblical order of the books which bear their names. As we read, we may slowly begin to notice how much these prophets differ from one another. Each of them has a distinct personality, defined through his family background and his character and the circumstances in which he lives. At the same time, however, all the prophets also have a good deal in common.

Each prophet certainly points towards the future, but they are concerned with something which they expect to happen very soon. By the time of the prophets, from about 750 BC onwards, the former kingdom of David had long been divided into two states, the northern kingdom of Israel and the much smaller southern kingdom of Judah, with Jerusalem as its capital. In both kingdoms, the ancient God of all Israel was worshipped as a national deity. It was common at the time for each nation to have its own God. The inhabitants of Israel and Judah looked to their God, whom they called Yahweh, for protection and for ever greater prosperity. They believed that he was a God who would bring salvation to his people. He had made himself known by freeing Israel from Egypt and guiding the people into their own land, and they expected that he would continue to act along these lines in the future. For he had bound himself to his people for all time, and he was greater and more power-ful than the gods of all the other nations. He was the only real and true God, so Israel and Judah could count on a happy future.

At this point, the prophets were those who took the opposite view. 'A happy future? No, no, no! Yahweh is going to bring disaster down on you. A special relationship with Israel? Yes, that may have been the case, but now Yahweh has done away with it.' Most of the prophets preached in this style. Each of them was overwhelmed by the reality of God. The average inhabitants of Judah and Israel had their faith by hearsay. They believed that Yahweh existed and had delivered his people from Egypt, that they were to worship him with sacrifices, that he had given them rules and laws and so on. They had learnt this from their parents, but did not trouble their heads about it. The prophets felt that they had been called by Yahweh himself. They did not know him by hearsay, or through an inherited belief, but directly. And the experience was shattering. The prophets were amazed that they were still alive. For Yahweh was so completely different from the common idea of him. 'Holy' is the prophets' word for him. The people thought that they were God's favourites, but how could that be? They perpetrated injustice and violence; the rich took houses and fields from the poor in order to have a monopoly of the land, and they called this wickedness good! They thought that they could guarantee their permanent welfare through sacrifices and the singing of psalms. 'No', said the prophets in the name of Yahweh, 'It is all up with Israel. I will not spare them any more.'

The prophets felt called to proclaim their message not only among the people, but also at the royal palace and in the temple of Yahweh. In this way they came up against resistance. It made them solitary men, with at best a few exceptional followers who sensed in them something of this God whose nature had to be different from what people imagined. The prophets did not have a pleasant life. They disagreed too strongly with the feelings and thoughts and expectations of others. They seemed to be madmen. First they were laughed at, then abused, persecuted and at times tortured and killed.

At a later date, the sayings of the prophets were collected together and written down, along with notes by others about their careers. These writings were added to the sacred books of the Jews. By reading them, people could get the impression that a prophet was someone who came up against resistance because of his message, and was mistreated and killed by his fellow-countrymen. Hence sayings like, 'A prophet is without honour in his own country.' In due course we shall see that Jesus was familiar with this idea. Meanwhile, we must spend a little longer with the ancient prophets, because we need to know still more about their work and their fortunes if we are to understand John the Baptist and Jesus.

The way in which I have described the message of the prophets sounds rather negative: 'The end of Israel is near, Yahweh has finished with his people.' I should also add that the prophets did speak positively about the future. However, their good news was for the time *after* the judgment, after disaster and annihilation. One might sum up their preaching rather like this: Yahweh can do no more with this Israel, but he can create a new people, and because his faithfulness is beyond all our imagining, this is what he will do. For he is God, and not man. So he can draw a line under the past, and give people a completely new chance. In our terms, that means forgiveness. God can forgive in a way which goes immeasurably far beyond our own understanding. Sometimes the prophets say that Yahweh will create the new people from a 'remnant', a small group of people who have survived the judgment and for whom it has brought purification rather than annihilation. Here we can recognize one feature of John the Baptist's message, and we can understand why people labelled him as a prophet.

The element of disaster in the preaching of the prophets did not come only from their direct experience of the holy God. National disaster was so to speak in the air. Even without a prophetic experience of the reality of God, people could have the feeling of impending doom. You really need to look at a map of the Middle East to understand why. Picture to yourself how the narrow strip of Palestine forms a link between Egypt in the south and the great areas of the north-east which are now Syria, Iraq and Iran. Israel and Judah, along with the small neighbouring states, were situated between these two super-powers. When the powers were in equilibrium, they could survive. But if one super-power grew much stronger than the other, then disaster and annihilation threatened. That happened in the eighth century BC. Assyria advanced to the coastal area, present-day Lebanon, and then pressed further south towards Egypt.

The prophets' forebodings were realized. In 721, the Assyrian armies wiped the northern kingdom of Israel off the map. The king, and those members of his court and of the upper classes who had not been killed, were deported to various parts of the Assyrian empire. There they lost all contact with their past and vanished for ever from history. The Assyrian empire was then menaced by a new power, Babylon, which in 612 captured the Assyrian capital Nineveh. In 597 it was the Babylonians who conquered the surviving kingdom Judah and its capital, Jerusalem, deporting the king and some of the leading citizens to Babylon. They set up a new king in Jerusalem, expecting that he would be a faithful vassal of Babylon and guard the important route to Egypt, but he rebelled, so in

25

587 the Babylonians made an end of the state of Judah. The leading citizens who survived were again deported to Babylon. As far as they were concerned that really did mean the end of Yahweh and his people. Everything that pointed to the covenant with him, their land, the Temple, the kingship of David and his followers, had been destroyed. The prophets had been right. What they had said in the name of Yahweh had now become harsh reality.

However, prophets also emerged among the people of Judah in Babylon. Now they no longer proclaimed the judgment, because that had taken place. Nor did they denounce all forms of social injustice, because there were no longer rich and poor, exploiters and oppressors: all the exiles from Judah were equally the victims. Nor did they need to go on pointing to the senselessness of temple worship with its sacrifices and its prayers, since the Temple of Jerusalem lay in ruins.

In the conditions of exile in Babylon the prophets again went against the stream, differing from the rest in their thoughts and feelings. Continuing the old conviction of Yahweh's faithfulness, they promised renewal. In those gloomy circumstances they proclaimed a new future in Yahweh's name. It seemed unbelievable. Against all appearances, they gave the assurance that Yahweh had not abandoned his people for ever. A mother might possibly forget her child, one of them said, but Yahweh had not forgotten his people. In their despair, the people of Judah and Jerusalem were saying to each other in Babylon; 'It is all up with us as a people. We are as good as dead, destroyed, a pile of dead bones in a desert valley.' Then the prophet Ezekiel related what he had seen in a moment of ecstasy: Yahweh had breathed his life-giving spirit upon the dead bones; flesh and muscle and sinews had come upon them, and the valley had gradually become full of a countless host of living people. Yahweh would return with his people to Jerusalem and he would gather together all those who had been dispersed, even the members of the former kingdom of northern Israel. The city would be rebuilt and he would rule there as king over his restored people. Everyone, from far and near, from the ends of the earth, would be amazed at the way in which Yahweh had

26

brought salvation to his people, and they would come to visit him in Israel bearing their treasures in reverent homage.

At this point I must end this hasty account of the 'classical' prophets. They felt themselves called by God, so they had to announce the threat of judgment over Israel as they saw it. At the same time, however, this same experience of God gave them a new perspective on the future, with the prospect of a completely changed world. Through 'conversion' and 'repentance' an individual could survive and have a share in the new age. This was the message of the prophets of the classical period, from about 750 to 550 BC. John the Baptist clearly stood in the same line, which is why people called him a prophet.

Still, five centuries separated John from these great figures, and during that time a good deal happened to make the position of John – and indeed of Jesus – quite different. The belief that I described above, in a restoration of Israel, a time when the people of Judah and Israel would again be gathered together, never came to anything. On the contrary, although a number of people from Judah returned home to their fatherland and their beloved city of Jerusalem after 538, at the end of the Babylonian captivity, most of them preferred to stay in Babylon. They had become accustomed to life there, and did not want to return to their ruined city, their shattered villages and estates, which by now were either desolate or occupied by strangers. Former inhabitants of Judah also went out from Babylon to other parts of the world. Sometimes, as for example in Egypt, they met fellow-countrymen who had emigrated at an earlier time.

After this period people from the former tribal territory and kingdom of Judah (Judaea) who had dispersed so widely over the world were given the name of Jews. Their belief in Yahweh and his faithfulness had to be expressed in new forms to match their new circumstances. We must look at two of these forms more closely. First, the Jews created the 'Torah' as a framework for their beliefs, and we shall see how Jesus came into conflict with it. Secondly, they continued to look for the 'restoration' in which they believed. Now, however, they expected it in a new world which was to come from God, who would make an end of this old world because he could no longer reign in it as king. The Jews, then, expected the coming of a 'kingdom of God'.

— 5 —

The Torah and the End of this World

The Jews who lived in and around Jerusalem and those who had settled a long way away, in Babylonia, Egypt and in the great cities elsewhere, had two things in common. They shared the same ancestors and they shared belief in the same God. However, they had to live their life among people with a different heritage and with very different ideas. These people had their local customs and institutions, their laws and their temples. The Jews were a small minority, even in Palestine. If they were not to forget their ancestry and thus to dissipate their faith, they needed a clear structure, a clear expression of their faith, and clear rules for their daily conduct. In other words, they needed a code of Jewish social ethics.

According to a trustworthy tradition, Ezra (or as his name was spelt in Greek, Esdras) created this structure round about the year 400 BC. Ezra lived in Babylon and was the specialist on Jewish affairs in the central Persian government. He was thoroughly familiar with the traditions which the Jews had preserved from their past, some of them in writing. Many of the documents were very old, and others which had been revised over the course of the centuries, even during the period of the captivity and afterwards, contained at least some old passages. Ezra collected all this material into one book. It came to be called the 'Torah'. In English, the word is usually rendered 'Law', but in one sense that is a misleading description, because the great book which Ezra compiled was made up of roughly the first five books in our Bibles, the 'books of Moses'. It is obvious to anyone that this collection contains a large number of stories: it begins with the creation of the world, tells the

29

story of paradise and the Fall and the tower of Babel, and then spends a long time on the adventures of Abraham, Isaac and Jacob. There follow the rescue of the Israelites from captivity in Egypt, the exodus and the stay in the wilderness, coming to a climax with the revelation of God on Sinai, the making of the covenant between Yahweh and his people and the giving of the law. From that point on, the element of law in fact takes up most of the following sections.

Nevertheless, it remains extremely significant that the law-giving as a whole was put in a narrative framework, and that the narrative really describes the Jewish view of life. For it tells how the world was made and why it exists, and also how the people of Israel were called to life by God and why they came into being. Thus 'Torah' means much more than law: it is really instruction, a rule for living, indeed what we might call a view of life, though with a very practical application. Here are guidelines for the Israelites to follow both as individuals and as a community, showing them how to behave as Yahweh wanted them to. This is why Ezra was called 'the father of Judaism'. And the day on which he came to read the Torah in Jerusalem to the assembled people is called 'the birthday' of Judaism.

People soon became convinced that Moses himself had written the Torah, and not Ezra. We find a good expression of the function that the books of Moses fulfilled among the Jews in a story which was written later by an Egyptian Jew. He put the following words into the mouth of the high priest in Jeru-salem: 'Our wise lawgiver, endowed by God with the knowledge of all things, has ringed us round with unbroken hedges and walls of iron, so that we do not mix with other people in any way, remaining pure in body and mind, delivered from worth-less opinions, worshipping only the one almighty God and nothing that has been made.'

The way in which the Torah shaped their social life set the Jews apart from the people around them. The Torah did in fact become as it were a hedge round the Jewish community, a dividing wall between them and all other men.

To understand why Jesus was soon regarded as a heretic and a blasphemer by the upright Jews of his time we need to note two developments in connection with the Torah. First, the book was talked about in increasingly reverent terms. People saw clearly how utterly important, how fundamental, how indispensable it was for the life of the Jews, who were God's people. They did not have words like 'important', 'fundamental', 'indispensable' in their language; their way of thinking differed from ours. Whenever a custom or a religious institution meant a great deal to them, they would describe how old it was. They would even claim that it had been instituted by a great figure from their past. One example of this is circumcision. When the remains of the people of Judah were deported to Babylon, they saw that circumcision was quite unusual there. It marked them out. So in Babylon circumcision became a token of the ancestry and belief that bound them together. They began to tell the story of how God had already required Abraham to be circumcised as a token of his covenant. The old custom of observing the seventh day, the sabbath, as a weekly festival, also acquired special significance in Babylon. Most other religious festivals had been associated with the Temple in Jerusalem, and so they could not be celebrated in Babylon. The sabbath, too, became — as we would put it — very important and was of fundamental significance. In order to express this deep conviction, the incomparably fine story, or better poem, of creation was put at the beginning of the Torah. God himself had observed the sabbath. He worked at the creation of the world for six days and rested on the seventh.

The Torah was even more important than circumcision or the sabbath; it was really more fundamental, the basis of all the institutions and customs which distinguished the Jews from other people, or to put it in modern terms, which gave identity to their community. So they developed the idea that God created the Torah before he began to make anything else, heaven or earth. The book was his first creation. This helps us to understand the answer to a question which is raised by the first pages of the Torah. They describe how God first began to make all kinds of animals on the sixth day of creation. Then he suddenly begins to speak in the plural: 'Let us now make man in our own image and likeness.' Why does he do that? Well, said some Jews, he was talking to the Torah!

In that case, of course, Moses was no longer the real author of the Torah. The heavenly texts were revealed to this greatest and holiest man of all time, and he copied them out accurately. Another similar idea was that a heavenly being, an angel, had dictated the sacred texts to Moses. This gave rise to the idea of a holy book, dictated to a sacred or 'inspired' writer. There are still Christians who look on their Bible in this way, as literally 'the word of God', entirely written by him from beginning to end.

I cannot say more here about the way in which the Jews expressed among themselves their deep reverence and admiration for the Torah. Outsiders saw only the unique way of life which they based on their holy book. The most striking features were their observation of the sabbath as a day of rest, their careful avoidance of 'unclean' food or drink or of contact with anything that made them unclean, and the circumcision of their male children. A century and a half before Christ, this mode of behaviour took on so to speak a new significance. It was 'hallowed' by the blood of martyrs. This is the second development which we must now consider, because it was still influential in the time of Jesus, shaping his own thoughts and feelings and those of the people among whom he moved.

A completely new life-style developed after Alexander the Great of Greece had conquered the greater part of the then known world and had even advanced some way towards India. When he died in 323 BC, in his thirty-third year, he had scarcely begun on the ambitious task he had set himself. For Alexander did not just want to be a rich and powerful ruler. He had a great ideal. He wanted to do away with all hostility between people and races by making all men Greeks. He wanted to make mankind one again, so that people everywhere would speak the same language and live and work in the same way. There was to be one culture and one religion for all. This plan would, of course, provoke the opposition of the Jewish community, which set itself apart from all other men. However, that did not happen during the short life of Alexander. He advanced through the coastal plain of Palestine on his triumphant expedition to Egypt, but in all probability he had barely heard of the ideas and life-style of the Jews who lived in and around Jerusalem, when his great army camped in the hill country there.

About a century and a half after Alexander's death, however, his ideal was opposed by the Jewish community in Palestine. The narrow rectangular strip of land along the coast had at that time come into the possession of the royal house which ruled over part of Alexander's empire. Its capital was Antioch, in the north. Antiochus IV was the first to come up against the Jews in Judaea. Characteristically, he had given himself the title Epiphanes, 'the one who appears in divine form'. He, too, tried to unify the great variety of ethnic groups within his territory on very much the same lines as Alexander. He encouraged people as much as he could to speak and write Greek and to live in accordance with Greek habits and customs. Unity of language and culture also meant unity of worship. Local gods were given the names of Greek gods, but Antiochus' subjects also had to recognize that he himself was a manifestation, a revelation of God.

Numerous people, above all educated people, had long been attracted by Alexander's ideal. The way of life which the Greeks, or Hellenes, brought with them, was always particularly attractive. It seemed really modern. There was an end to the pettiness of provincial existence, with all its links to a gloomy past; there were no longer quarrels with other groups in the neighbourhood. No, once one began to think and feel in a Greek way, the whole world, the whole of mankind became one's home. The old narrow-minded thinking of one's forefathers gave way to a new broad outlook, the reflections of the greatest and wisest philosophers which Greece had produced on man and nature and the world. A new style of building developed, with porticoes and colonnades and fountains. There were temples for the old gods in their new garb. As Greek culture gained a footing in a country, it seemed as though a new, fresh wind was beginning to blow. People went to the theatres which seemed to mushroom up everywhere. Young men went to the splendid stadiums to take part in athletics or to wrestle, which they did in the nude. It was all glorious, natural and free.

Many Jews came under the spell of the new and modern way of life. Above all, those who lived close to Hellenistic cities, or had to go there on business, became rather ashamed of their own customs. To spend one whole day out of seven doing nothing at all, staying put, not even carrying anything around, while everyone else went on with their exciting new life, seemed absurd. Not to eat delicacies which were offered by friends or served in restaurants because they were unclean really seemed to be an old taboo. Men who went swimming or took part in games were ashamed of being circumcised. And the rebuilt Temple in Jerusalem, of which the Jews had once been so proud, was really not very impressive when set alongside the gleaming new buildings with their porticoes and their colonnades. Above all, it had no statues! In the inner sanctuary of the Temple in Jerusalem, where Greek temples would have a splendid statue of the deity, was nothing but a pitch-dark room, with absolutely nothing in it. It seemed much better for those who had an eye to the future, and wanted to be really open to the whole of mankind, really modern, to break away from their narrow and restricted past with its bizarre regulations and taboos.

However, there were also Jews who held on fiercely to the old ways, the legacy of their fathers, and wanted to preserve them at any price. Antiochus IV came up against them in about 170 BC. He tried to use force to make those Jews who were faithful to the Law adopt Greek customs and brought in police and troops to implement his policy. Some Jews were compelled to eat swine's flesh, and if they persistently refused, they were killed. Mothers who had had their children circumcised were tortured. The same fate befell those who were found in possession of a copy of the Torah. Many Jews resorted to arms to defend themselves. But on the sabbath they were not allowed to carry anything, and that included weapons. So if they were attacked on that day, they were defenceless, and were ruthlessly slaughtered. Their first great leader was Judas the Maccabean, who was later succeeded by some of his brothers.

Meanwhile Antiochus had gone as far as attacking the Jews at their most sensitive point, their 'holy of holies'; he occupied the Temple in Jerusalem and sent his soldiers into the dark sanctuary where God dwelt. Indeed, he went even further and had a statue of Olympian Zeus set up in the temple, which may perhaps have been in some respects a self-portrait.

Pious Jews found it hard to imagine any greater monstrosity. This was the end. Now the God of Israel would have to appear in majesty as ruler of the world, and at a stroke he would destroy all evildoers and idolaters and their kingdoms. The end of the godless world was inevitable.

This conviction was no novelty to the Jews, but in the dispute with Antiochus it acquired new life and continued to be influential down to the time of Jesus and even afterwards. We must therefore pause to consider it for a moment.

We have already seen that at the time of the Babylonian captivity and shortly afterwards the prophets had spoken of a future restoration of Jerusalem. From the city, Yahweh would reign as king over his own people and over all other nations: he would be the sole ruler of the whole world. These expectations were expressed in visions and poems of all kinds; people could read the texts in the prophetic books, which began to acquire the holiness of the Torah, the holy book *par excellence*.

However, things did not turn out like that. Jerusalem remained an insignificant city. Control over the world as it was then known lay first in the hands of the Persians, and then with Alexander and his successors. In the second century, Palestine watched a new world power emerge, that of Rome. All the important decisions about the nations were made far outside Jerusalem. The city was not involved in any way, except in the hearts of the Jews, most of whom lived far away, somewhere in the wider world. Many of them also had a strong sense of their own sinfulness, and of the need for penitence and reconciliation. So at the beginning of the second century BC we can see how certain groups became convinced that Yahweh would not be able to establish his kingdom in the world as it now was. There was no longer any point of contact for him; the world had become too evil and corrupt. If Yahweh was to establish his kingdom, as he would, he would have to create a completely new world. Only a world like that, quite different from the world as it was, could correspond with the God who is

35

utterly perfect. Only a world like that could be 'holy', i.e. completely different. God would have to put an end to the present world, because it was evil through and through, and he would do that very soon. With the defilement committed by Antiochus, wickedness really had reached a peak. No greater abomination was conceivable.

The expectation of what would happen 'very soon' gave rise to a remarkable kind of literature called 'apocalyptic', 'books of revelation'. These books are difficult for us to understand, much less evaluate, but they were loved by many Jews and give us some idea of the thoughts and feelings of some of Jesus' contemporaries.

God had, of course, foreseen all the misery which the Jews now had to endure, as he had foreseen all the earlier disasters. It was obvious, therefore, that everyone involved was playing a part which God had chosen for him beforehand. In view of God's omnipotence and omniscience, world history could only develop in accordance with the plans which he had made from the beginning. The imminent destruction of all evil and the establishment of his eternal rule had also been decreed from all eternity. God could, of course, have communicated his plans to people long ago and this was the possibility which the apocalyptic writers made use of to express their conviction and their hope. The patriarch Enoch was an obvious candidate for receiving revelations from God. He was the seventh in the series between Adam and Noah, and the Torah records that when he was 365 years old he did not die, but was transported to heaven by God. It was thought that he could have written what God had shown him about the distant future and a book of visions was attributed to him. The fiction that Enoch himself had written the book also implied that it had remained 'hidden' down the centuries, and had only now been revealed by the writer. Moses, too, was thought a likely recipient of visions of the future, as were Isaiah and other prophets.

Such books of revelations were still being written in the time of Jesus, and they were eagerly read in certain circles. As time went on, the Jews stopped copying most of them because they were no longer interested, so their original texts were lost. It was

36

only during the last century that some of them were rediscovered, as a whole or in part, in translations made by the early churches. Fortunately one such book found a place in the Jewish Bible, our Old Testament, so that anyone who wants to, may form some idea of this remarkable kind of literature and discover the thoughts and expectations expressed in it, which so occupied the minds of Jesus' contemporaries.

I am now referring to the book of Daniel. We know that it was written during the terrible years when Antiochus was trying to force the Jews to give up their distinctive way of life. So the writer begins with stories about a certain Daniel and three other men of Judah who many years before had come to Babylon, and its powerful royal court. The rulers of Babylon tried to persuade Daniel and his companions to give up their Jewish faith and life-style. They failed to do this, because God rescued the Jews out of the fiery furnace and out of the lion's den. Daniel is kept informed of God's plans and knows the future of the godless rulers and their empires. The writer makes him describe how he sees future events in visions. The rulers of the world powers will grow steadily worse, and the last of them will desecrate God's temple. That will be the end, because at that point God will intervene, put an end to evil and its power, and hand over the whole world to a new ruler, a mysterious heavenly figure in the likeness of a man, a 'Son of man'. An angel then explains to Daniel that the Son of man is a symbol for those Jews who are faithful to the Law, who will have a part in God's eternal rule, the kingdom of God.

The writer also expressed his belief that those Jews who were faithful to the Law and who died for their faith will have a part in this great future. It is worth remembering that here, in the book of Daniel, we find for the first time in the Old Testament a clear expression of the expectation of a resurrection of the dead, as part of what God will accomplish when he puts an end to this evil world and establishes his kingdom.

— 6 —

Jesus Goes his own Way

Many children are still taught that before the time of Jesus *the* Jews were expecting *the* Messiah. Such a comment ought to be removed from school textbooks once and for all, and it should certainly never be made in sermons. First, because it is usually the prelude to saying that Jesus was the looked-for Messiah, and that leads to the unpleasant conclusion that it was very wicked of the Jews to put their Messiah to death. The facts should be presented differently, so as not to suggest such a consequence. But secondly, above all, because it is not true that *the* Jews were looking for *the* Messiah. People in Palestine at that time had a variety of different expectations. John had his own ideas, as we have seen, and so did Jesus.

It is difficult for us to get a clear idea of the general situation. What people hope for and expect always depends on the circumstances in which they find themselves. In the Palestine of the first century the situation was very confused for everyone. We have seen the hopes of the pious writer of the book of Daniel a century and a half earlier: he expected that within a very short space of time God would put an end to all evil powers and would then establish his kingdom, which would be eternal and everlasting and would bring happiness to all pious Jews. However, this hope was disappointed and instead of the unchallenged rule of God and his faithful, bad governments persisted, their rulers became worse and worse, and misery deepened. The Maccabees fought so that the Jews might have freedom to live in accordance with the Torah. That was good, but their successors made themselves not only high priests but also very worldly rulers. This deeply offended the true believers among their subjects, who banded together in groups, 'parties', like the Pharisees. Others escaped from godless Jerusalem and went into the wilderness around the banks of the Dead Sea. These Essenes, as they were called, began to form a priestly community, on the basis of the Torah, with the strictest possible emphasis on 'purity'.

With bad governments and a divided population, Palestine became an easy prey for the Romans. They regarded it as a district of Syria which they wanted to incorporate into their empire. It is difficult to summarize in a sentence or two the course of events from the day in 63 BC when the Roman general Pompey arrived in Palestine with his army, to the time when Jesus appeared on the scene. We cannot overestimate the complexity of the situation, or exaggerate the violence of the tensions between all the different groups in tiny Palestine. Nowhere were they more marked than in Jerusalem, which was capital of Judaea and, at the same time, because of its Temple, a kind of meeting place for Jews from outside Judaea. They came there from the farthest corners of the world. On any day it will have been possible to hear at least four languages being spoken in the city. Aramaic was the everyday language of the ordinary Jew. It differed from ancient Hebrew rather as Dutch differs from German. Hebrew was the language of the Torah and the other holy books. It was the language many people used for their daily prayers, while priests and scribes also used it whenever they discussed religious matters and the Torah. A good many educated Jews wrote and spoke Greek, even at home. Greek was the language of much of the civilized world, widely used in trade and commerce. It will have been spoken by the majority of Jews living in the Diaspora, outside Palestine. Some families had come from the Greek-speaking Diaspora and had settled in Jerusalem. They did not take the trouble to learn the local Aramaic.

Latin, too, was spoken in Jerusalem as the language of the Roman rulers, officials and soldiers. The permanent residence of the governor, who at the time of Jesus was Pontius Pilate (AD 26–36), was in the attractive city of Caesarea (Caesar's city) on the Mediterranean coast. Particularly during the great feasts, however, he came to Jerusalem with his troops in order to strengthen the garrison there. Military occupation of a country provokes resistance and introduces new tensions. It also gives rise to the most varied expectations.

The older ones among us can remember this from 1940 and the years that followed. Those who had a big business, a building firm or a grocery store, or those who held public office, like mayors, were faced with difficult decisions. Should they utterly refuse to collaborate with the Germans and see what happened? Should they profit from the new situation and make the most of it? Or should they concede just enough to save a large number of fellow-countrymen from a worse situation? A man could go his own quiet way, trying not to attract attention by outright disobedience to the new law, or he could join the underground resistance movement. He could think, 'The Germans are not so bad after all, and in any case they have brought law and order, perhaps even more successfully than some of our so-called democratic governments.' Or he could regard their presence as intolerable, like a plague or a cancer to be fought against with every means possible. His choice would depend to a great deal on his past and on his position, on whether he had thought much about improving society or whether he had lived only for himself, on whether he had a lot to lose or not much.

People's attitudes would also determine the way in which they regarded the prospect of liberation. Those who had been open supporters of the Germans would look to it with fear and trembling, those who had suffered under the occupation would look forward to it with deep longing, while those who had starved over the previous winter could hardly wait for it to come.

At this point we discover the reasons why this illustration does not quite fit. There was one enormous difference between the occupation of Holland during the war years and the Roman occupation of Palestine: for the Jews there was no chance of liberation. There was no other power in the world which could take on Rome, as the Allies took on the Germans.

'But that's where you're wrong,' said the Jews. 'There is such a power, but it is not of this world. It is the power of our God, the Lord of the heavenly hosts. He will free his people and destroy the might of Rome.'

However, by no means all Jews had equally strong faith and hope, just as not all Dutchmen looked forward to liberation with equal longing. Rich men, landowners, members of the priestly nobility and others did not find conditions too bad under Roman rule. There can be advantages when the military preserve law and order; it gives one a feeling of security. The Jews who had the right to collect the taxes imposed by the Romans thought very much in this way. They profited from the occupation and hoped that it would go on for ever. By contrast, it was the countless victims of exploitation, the wage-earners and the poor, who had eager expectations of divine intervention. God was the only power able to free them from their oppressors, the Romans and all who profited from Roman rule.

Among these oppressed people, expectations were rife. Would God himself intervene? Or would he raise up a leader from among the people, a king like David, his 'anointed', i.e. Messiah, who would annihilate the oppressors with divine power? Was it not possible to encourage divine action by preparing armed resistance, underground?

Ordinary citizens and tradespeople also had a deep longing for liberation from the Romans, but this had a more positive tone. It was a religious longing for the time when God would reign alone. Everyone could do something towards it; they could bring about God's reign now in some respect by obeying him in all things: his will would then be done on earth as in heaven. God reigned wherever his words were obeyed. In these circles, most influence was exercised by the party of Pharisees with their deep concern for life in accordance with the Torah and their scrupulous observance of all commandments and prohibitions.

The rich priestly families had little desire for liberation. The God of Israel was worshipped in his Temple, through all kinds of sacrifices and liturgies, each of which was controlled down to the smallest detail. This, they thought, was as it ought to be.

It is understandable that the Roman authorities did not interfere with Jewish religious life, except when it aroused 'messianic' expectations among the poor and oppressed, especially in Galilee. In this open and friendly landscape people had a more fiery temperament and were easier to arouse than the dour inhabitants of the difficult hill country around the capital. It happened more than once that a Galilean would lead a troop of locals to Jerusalem in order to bring in God's reign there. The Romans then came down on them with great severity. They sometimes nailed up groups of rebels on crosses around the capital.

The Roman police therefore kept a sharp look out whenever they heard that someone had gathered a following and was stirring people up about the kingdom of God. The Jews could reflect on the law to their heart's content, considering all kinds of nuances, but the police were quite clear on one thing: any movement which talked about the rule of God, his 'judgment' or 'reign', was *per se* anti-Roman. In view of the tense situation, a small movement could prove the spark that set the whole mass of the people ablaze.

So what John the Baptist did was dangerous. In fact it cost him his life. The area along the Jordan was under the jurisdiction of Herod Antipas, who had been appointed by the Romans. John was arrested by the king's police and later executed in prison. It seems most likely that Antipas thought that by acting in this way he was doing a good turn to his Roman masters.

We have seen that Jesus had attached himself to John. We should very much like to know whether it was after the arrest of his master that Jesus began to preach on his own account, taking up where John had been compelled to leave off. Or had the two men parted company at an early stage? Unfortunately we have no information. In any case, as we meet Jesus at the beginning of his dangerous task, we can see marked similarities to John along with even more striking differences. Jesus himself had been influenced by John's summons: 'Repent quickly! Judgment is near! Seize your last chance! Be baptized by me as a sign of your conversion!' Jesus had therefore resolved to devote himself completely to what was to come. When he began to preach on his own account, he repeated John's urgent cry: 'Repent and do not wait any longer! The time is short!'

However, one gets the impression that Jesus' summons

sounded even more urgent than that of John. Jesus could not be content to wait by the Jordan. John had spoken there to Jews who had had to come to him. He had to wait until they bothered to make the journey. Jesus evidently did not want to wait. He travelled through Jewish territory, from village to village, from town to town, calling on people to repent. It was clear that he wanted to reach as many Jews as possible, as quickly as possible, so he went to seek them out wherever they lived and worked. That was also why he was quick to enlist the help of others. He was in such a hurry. Every Jew had to have a chance, a last chance.

Jesus, then, seems to have had a somewhat greater sense of urgency than John, and in any case felt more impelled to go to his fellow-countrymen. But there is another difference in the summons proclaimed by the two men, which is perhaps of decisive significance. John pointed towards the immediate future, to what was going to happen very soon. 'The axe is laid at the root of the tree. Look out, it is coming very soon!' Jesus seemed to say, 'Look, the matter is even more urgent. What John announced is happening *now*! God is coming now!'

Jesus fills the word 'God', so to speak, with new meaning. This is how he evidently feels the presence of God, experiences him, draws life from him. God is a power who is ready to give unconditionally, to forgive, to heal, to create new chances, for anyone, without distinction and without limit, now. Jesus seem ed to be utterly possessed by this God. Like John, he too expected a 'judgment', apparently very soon. However, this judgment was to be no more than a confirmation of the way in which men reacted now to the God whom Jesus believed to be at work, a continuation of their reaction to his own words and deeds.

There was another difference. John made a demand on people when they heeded his call for repentance: they had to submit to his baptism in the Jordan. Jesus did not ask what sort of man you were. He simply gave. Proclaiming that his God was now at work, he made him visible and tangible. People heard God preached and saw him in action: the lame began to walk again, the blind received their sight, lepers were healed, broken relationships between men were restored, the possessed were freed from their evil spirits.

Jesus was evidently driven on by his God and possessed by him. He was also delighted that he could make God so audible and so visible. Without being arrogant or pretentious, he felt that people who met him were extremely lucky. He used to say this, or rather, he almost sang it in joy: 'Kings and prophets have longed to see what you now see, but they did not see it; and to hear what you now hear, but they did not hear it.' The kings and prophets had looked out for the day of God, the day on which he would make all things 'whole' and realize his salvation. Jesus said that this day had now dawned. The rule of God, his 'kingdom' which previously had been looked for in the future, had begun. The previous period had come to an end with John the Baptist. Jesus calls him the greatest man who ever lived. But that was in the period which had now ended; and now the simplest man who heeded Jesus' God was 'greater than John'.

Jesus himself claimed that he brought people what they and their forefathers had wanted. Yet they did not accept him. How did that come about? Was he deluding himself? Was he the victim of his own dreams and illusions? Or could the people, for all their longings, manage to see what he really wanted?

$$\sim 7 \sim$$

'A New Teaching with Authority!'

Whenever I try to describe the impression Jesus made on people I get interrupted at every turn. Sometimes I can hear and see that the questioners are very agitated. My way of speaking has obviously disconcerted them. At first they thought that they were listening to a believer, but what they expected, a clear testimony to my belief in the divinity of Christ, never came, so they interrupt me in order to hear it, if only to discover how to assess me.

As the conversation goes on, it turns out that they could not recognize their own idea of the God-man in my description of Jesus. The important thing for them was that Jesus, simply because he was also God, had much greater power and knowledge than an ordinary person. For example, he changed more than a hundred gallons of water into the best wine without even saying a word. He cured sick men simply by touching them, and sometimes at a distance, without even doing that. He raised the dead to life, and they were real corpses, not people in a trance. The body of Lazarus had been buried for three days and stank. In a case like this only the Creator himself can restore life. The greatest miracle that Jesus did was to rise from the dead himself. He had foretold it, and that also proved that he was God: he knew in advance what was going to happen. Moreover, it was precisely because he was God that his sacrifice on the cross was so infinitely precious and has the atoning power which is all we need for being reconciled to God, in spite of our sins.

I imagine that a good many Christians still cherish such an idea of Jesus. This is unfortunate, because Jesus certainly never gave his followers the impression of being a God-man. We know this from the reminiscences that they have left us. We have fragmentary evidence of their reactions to being with him, and if we read them carefully and patiently, we shall find that they present a clear figure to us. He is not the God-man he is usually supposed to be, but an exceptional personality, at the same time both attractive and mysterious, indeed so bewildering that no one can really understand him. 'What is this?' said the people when Jesus came to them with his message, 'A new teaching with authority!' We have already discussed the new element in his teaching: he proclaimed that the kingdom of God, for which all previous generations had longed, had now dawned; God was beginning to reign and that was good news for everyone. According to the people, Jesus proclaimed this new message 'with authority'. We can see what they meant by that if we listen to the earliest evidence.

In our society, someone's words have authority when the person in question holds a particular office, exercises a particular function or has letters after his name. So a statement by the Queen, or by the Pope, or by a Fellow of the British Academy, or by a television personality carries special weight. Things were just the same in Jewish society, certainly in questions about God and his purpose for his people, about how Jews should behave and what they might expect. Only the religious authorities, priests, rabbis and scribes, could speak authoritatively here. They had long steeped themselves in the Torah and in the numerous traditions; after years of experience they had mastered Jewish doctrine and had acquired the competence to instruct others.

Jesus was not a priest or anything like that; he was an ordinary 'layman'. He had not been taught by rabbis, and he had no official authority to speak about God and his will.

Hence the amazement of the people of Nazareth, where he was known best. 'Where does he get it from? We know him and his family, his parents and brothers and sisters!' Later on, some of his disciples remembered what was said about him in his village: 'He has gone mad!' His mother and his brothers once went after him, evidently to try and bring him to his senses. Perhaps they spoke to him along these lines: 'What's this idea that's got into

46

your head? Stop confusing people with your rubbish about the kingdom of God! Come back home and just be a carpenter. Do what God wants in your ordinary everyday life. That's the important thing. Leave the coming of his kingdom to him. That's his business. Don't imagine that you, an ordinary young man, can do anything about it. Why are you getting our family talked about all round the village? It's much better for you and for everyone else to lead an ordinary life among us . . .!'

His family were right in thinking Jesus crazy, and at the same time he was extremely presumptuous. He felt called to win over 'all Israel' for his God, with the emphasis on 'his'. He felt a sense of great urgency, so he went from one village to another, in order that as many people as possible might hear and see what it really meant for his God to be near. He required people everywhere to make up their minds, asking them to adopt a completely new attitude. His God wanted to bring happiness to everyone, no matter what their past. All that his God asked for was unlimited trust. People were to trust God, and also their neighbours, indeed everyone whom they met, even those whom they regarded as good-for-nothings. They were even to trust their avowed enemies, because God trusted them, too.

This was quite a challenge, especially since Jesus required this new attitude of *all* Jews. It did not matter to what group or party they belonged, or what their place in society might be. He addressed them all, the punctiliously religious Jews and those who did not toe the line; the good patriots and the traitors; high and low, rich and poor, the respectable and the outcast. All the differences between the Jews, all the labels, the various distinctions, belonged to the past. Now God was coming. He was calling all his people, irrespective of their background, and inviting them all to the great feast, to be with him for ever.

According to Jesus, there was no time to lose. People could not delay over this new attitude; they could not put off conversion and repentance. That applied to every Jew. Because the time was so short, and the call had to reach everyone, Jesus enlisted helpers. He formed a group of twelve. This was the distinctive number of the ancient people of God, which was made up of twelve tribes. Jesus' choice of twelve must have suggested that God was now truly concerned with 'all Israel', with all the Jews. Jesus' intentions could also be seen from the composition of the group. There were one or two fishermen, people who had left their work on the Sea of Galilee to help Jesus with his mission; there was a tax-collector in the service of Rome, a 'publican'; and the group certainly included at least one 'zealot'. Thinking back to the German occupation of Holland, we might say that the group included a profiteer, far worse than a quisling, and a good patriot, perhaps even a member of the resistance. The word zealot means 'fanatic'. In Jesus' day the epithet could be applied to someone who not only lived in strict accordance with the Torah but also tried as hard as possible to make other Jews do the same. Such a person would of course be violently anti-Roman, even if he were not actively involved in the armed resistance movement.

It is possible that Judas was someone like this, zealous for the Torah and won over by Jesus to a completely new attitude, acceptance of the God who sought everyone's happiness. Jesus was more certain of this God than of anything that might be found in the Torah. Perhaps Judas was so deeply attached to the Torah that he felt that Jesus was going too far, and in the end did precisely what the Torah commanded in such a situation: anyone who teaches against the precepts of the Law must be handed over to the authorities. But this is only a guess. We have no certain knowledge of Judas' motives.

It is, however, certain that Jesus said and did things which were not in accord with the Law. People often asked him with what authority he acted. They wanted him to account for himself. If he had a clear commission from the God whom he preached, he ought to prove it. As the earliest evidence relates, people wanted Jesus to give 'a sign from heaven'. By that they meant an obvious miracle, an overwhelming revelation, a glimpse of God's glory, accompanied by a heavenly voice – in any case an unmistakable sign that God was behind him.

They felt that Jesus really should give such a proof. 'If you are truly acting on behalf of the God of Israel, then he must be able to do for you what he did for Moses, Aaron, Elijah and so

48

many others.' 'No,' said Jesus, '*my* God is not like that. He shows himself only to those who trust in him, to those who accept my message without any proof.'

In this connection he referred to the prophet Jonah. Every Jew knew the story of Jonah, the man who was rescued in the mouth of an enormous fish, and who then went on to preach in the great city of Nineveh. All he said was, 'Forty days, and Nineveh will be destroyed.' So the story goes. Jonah did not point to any divine authorization, he did not produce any arguments and he did not do any miracles. The people of Nineveh had only his message to go on. That is what Jesus seems to have meant by 'the sign of Jonah'. It was all that people were going to have; there would be nothing but his summons.

Those who still cling to the old idea of Jesus as the God-man might have an objection at this point: 'But Jesus did perform sensational miracles to authenticate his calling and his divine status.' However, they would be wrong. Jesus did not perform any miracles with this intention, though it is clear that people thought of him as a miracle-worker who had superhuman powers. He certainly 'drove out devils', as they said in those days, and cured all kinds of sickness. Along with most of his Jewish contemporaries, Jesus thought of sickness and afflictions which cut people off from society as the work of evil spirits, of the devil, Satan, Beelzebub or whatever their chief might be called. The innumerable evil spirits were a well-organized force, and wherever God began to rule, the powers of evil were driven back.

One might almost say that people pictured a tremendous struggle between two powers, two spheres of influence. Jesus obviously felt that his appearance on the scene was the prelude to the final overthrow of the powers of evil. His disciples remembered one of his sayings: 'I saw Satan cast out of heaven like a flash of lightning.' Wherever Jesus proclaimed the imminent reality of God's reign, he also as it were demonstrated this reality by actually repelling the power of Satan. He did this by winning over all kinds of people to his own sphere of influence; he freed them, body and spirit, making them once again healthy, acceptable members of human society. 'If I by the finger of God cast out devils, then the kingdom of God has really come among you.' But this was not a proof of his calling. Many rabbis and pious Jews had a reputation for casting out devils and healing the sick. Moreover, Jesus simply seemed to have superhuman powers; they need not necessarily have come from God. Hence the remarkable discussion which we find even in the earliest reminiscences. People who could not take Jesus asserted that he cast out devils by the power of Beelzebub, their chief. Jesus showed them the oddness of such an accusation. They should have known how well organized the power of Beelzebub was. The devil would not cut his own throat. Moreover, since there were pious Jews who also cast out devils, in whose power did they do that?

It seems very strange to modern people to talk about the devil and his organization. But here and in other eye-witness reminiscences we cannot fail to be struck by the complete assurance of Jesus. He was confident that through his own words and actions God was at work establishing the supremacy of goodness, and he was so sure of this that there was no room for doubt or uncertainty on his part. He did not let anything distract him from his task. This, too, must have impressed those who remembered that he acted 'with authority'.

For many of us, this word 'authority' is far from attractive. We do not like what we call 'authoritarian personalities'. On the whole, people of this kind have a very high opinion of themselves. They also tend to impose their wills on others. They find compulsion necessary because compulsion is the only way of achieving the law and order which are necessary for a prosperous society.

One can often sense some resistance even to the authority associated with Jesus. A student once interrupted me by saying, 'How can I feel anything about someone who thought himself so important? It's always I, I, I. I am the way, the truth and the life . . . I am the good shepherd . . . I am the resurrection and the life. And so it goes on.'

After some discussion, two things soon became clear. First, Jesus never in fact talked about himself like this. These statements were attributed to him by John the evangelist. John wrote about sixty years after the death of Jesus, and he had good reasons for putting such remarks on the lips of Jesus. Secondly, the people who were with Jesus took precisely the opposite view: as they remembered things, it was remarkable how little Jesus talked about himself. We have already seen how he congratulated those who were able to share the new way of life which began with his appearance: 'You are lucky to be able to see and hear what you do!' Not, 'You are lucky to be with *me*.' When John the Baptist was in prison, he is said to have sent people to Jesus to ask him, 'Are you the one who is to come, or should we look for another?' The answer which Jesus gave was not, 'Tell John that I am the one', but, 'Tell John what is happening: the blind see, the lame walk and the poor have the good news preached to them . . .' Jesus himself was sure that God was now decisively at work among his people. To convince his hearers of this and to penetrate their incomprehension, like John he pointed to the coming judgment. When history finally came to an end, the people of Nineveh would condemn Jesus' contemporaries 'because they repented at the preaching of Jonah, and behold, something greater than Jonah is here.' The Queen of Sheba would condemn the Jews who did not heed Jesus, 'because she came from afar to hear the wisdom of Solomon, and behold, something greater than Solomon is here . . .' Jesus did not say, 'I am more important than Solomon or Jonah, *I* am a more decisive sign,' or something of that kind. The decisive sign was what God was doing with people there and then.

Jesus was evidently very restrained about his own role. It seems as though he gave himself a subordinate position in the great encounter which was taking place between God and man. Perhaps this explains the irritation with which he rejected any title or qualification. 'Good master,' began someone who wanted to put a question to him. Jesus almost snapped back, 'Please do not call me good. God alone is good.'

One has the impression that Jesus wanted to highlight the essential point. People were to pay attention to God and not to him, but the God whom they were to heed was God as Jesus experienced and proclaimed him, the God who was deeply concerned with everyone's happiness.

This is why Jesus cared for everyone, in a way which was particularly striking when those for whom he showed his care were the outcasts of society. This fact emerges from many of the short stories which the first Christians told about him. We can easily misunderstand them if we are still thinking in terms of the God-man: Jesus healed all kinds of sick people, showing once again that he was capable of more than any ordinary man. It would be better to say that Jesus was engaged in something which other people had unfortunately not got round to doing.

When we read or listen to these stories, it is important for us to remember that in the society of the time even devout people regarded the sick as men apart. Lepers were 'unclean'. So were women with haemorrhages. The law of God forbade contact with such people. The lame and the blind were also avoided. Deaf and dumb people were outcasts from society precisely because of their ailments. All the physical conditions that we regard as 'handicaps' were regarded by the pious men of the time as consequences of sin and guilt. They were a divine punishment, a clear sign that God had rejected such men and written them off.

Many of the brief accounts of Jesus' actions show how he paid special attention to these people. He looked at them, took notice of them and gave them the feeling that they were accepted, that they were worthwhile. Then, by healing them, he gave them a real chance to join in with others, to be members of society. He thought and acted in a very different way from the really religious people around him. They judged everything and everyone in accordance with the Torah and the usual theological notions about blessings and curses, which were seen as ways in which God showed his pleasure and his wrath.

Jesus thought about things in quite another way. He obviously experienced God very differently, and tried to convey his experience to others. It made him very happy, and happiness is something to be shared.

That is why Jesus tried to break through the familiar patterns. He did so with his special concern for the outcast, who were always victims of the old patterns of thinking and judging.

He also did so with his teaching. One characteristic of this is again his concern – and respect – for those with whom he was speaking. In contrast to the religious experts of his time he asked people for their own opinions. He appealed to their insight and their common sense. He preferred to give them a choice rather than overwhelm them with an argument. If you compare Christian reminiscences of Jesus' teaching with what we know about the usual teaching methods of that time, you will see why people spoke of a 'new' teaching with authority.

I shall mention only the parables here. According to those who are well-versed in world literature, Jesus was an undisputed master of this genre. To put it briefly, parables are stories, usually very short, which describe a particular situation or event so as to arouse the hearer's imagination: the story makes him think and forces him to look at his own situation with new eyes, to consider it from an unaccustomed perspective.

For example, the righteousness of God played a considerable part in Jewish thought and belief. God rewarded good deeds and punished evil deeds in accordance with a strict code. We have already seen how many people became the victims of this way of thinking. Jesus seems to have disagreed with it strongly. In his view, God had begun a completely new age. What had happened earlier no longer counted with God. What mattered was that now, in this new situation which Jesus was announcing and bringing about, people should turn to his God. Just imagine: it did not matter if you had never observed the law, had collaborated with the Romans, had extorted money from fellow Jews, had resorted to prostitutes, or whatever. You only had to turn to Jesus' God and then everything would be all right! You would be as near to God as the person who had lived according to the Torah from his youth up, who had refrained from all these things in order to be obedient to God and to do what was right, difficult though that might often have been. It all seemed very unfair. Moreover, where would such ideas end? It would be extremely dangerous for ordinary people if this kind of thinking were generally accepted.

To those who thought and felt in this way Jesus told the story of the landowner who went early in the morning to hire workers for his vineyard. He agreed to pay them the usual daily wage, 'a penny' as it then was (ten pounds might be nearer the mark now!). Three hours later he went back again and saw a number of people standing unemployed in the market place. 'Come to work in my vineyard, too, and I will pay you the usual wage.' He went back after six hours and then after nine. Towards evening, about an hour before the end of the working day, he went yet again to the market place and again found men standing there unemployed. They said that no one had hired them. The employer also took them for his vineyard. When the day was over, the steward had to pay wages to all the workers. He began with those who had come to work last, and gave each of them a penny. Those who had been at work since early morning expected to get more, but they too got the agreed wage of a penny. Then they began to protest to the landowner and said, 'These lazy men who came last have worked only one hour, and you have given them just as much as those of us who have borne the burden and heat of the day.' Then the landowner said to one of those who protested, 'Friend, I do you no wrong. You agreed with me for a penny. Take what is owed you and go on your way. I want to give those who came last the same amount as you. Can't I do what I want with my own money? Or are you cross because I am generous?'

The question is left open for the audience. There was already considerable indignation about what Jesus preached. Surely it was against the doctrine of God's righteousness? Hence the fury. But . . . is that the real reason? Is the objection not rather to the thought that God really is as Jesus proclaimed him, unexpectedly good to people who according to the conventional way of thinking do not deserve it? Perhaps we cannot accept that God favours other people. Perhaps zeal for the purity of the law is a symptom of jealousy, a petty narrow-mindedness that grudges widespread pleasure. Perhaps God is very different, much greater than we thought, with an astonishing and incomprehensible goodness which does not fit into *our* ideas of righteousness.

The famous parable of the prodigal son was clearly meant to start its audience thinking in this way, or rather to invite them to abandon their usual attitudes. The younger of two sons goes to squander his inheritance in a foreign country. When he has nothing left, a famine breaks out and he finds himself in the most wretched state: he can only earn a living by looking after pigs, which people keep in that unclean land, and he is not even allowed to eat the husks on which the pigs are fed. Then he feels sorry and thinks of his father. He wants to go home, and knows what he will say: 'Father, I have wronged both God and you; I am no longer worthy to be called your son, but accept me as one of your labourers.' He goes back home. His father has evidently been keeping a lookout all the time. When he sees him coming a long way off he feels very sorry for him. He does what a respectable and well-bred man of the East would never do, and runs up to him. He falls on his neck and kisses him warmly. The son begins to make his prepared speech: 'Father, I have wronged both God and you: I am no longer worthy to be called your son . . .' But the father will not let him continue, and orders his servants to prepare a great feast and to treat his son as an honoured guest. Then the older brother comes back from working on the land. He hears music and dancing. When he discovers that the feast is because his brother has come back, he gets cross and does not want to join in. Then his father comes out and invites him in, but he retorts very crossly, 'All these years I have been working for you, I never disobeyed you, but you never even gave me food for a party with my friends. And now this son of yours has come back after squandering your money on evil women, and you have gone and killed the fatted calf for him.' The bit about the evil women is pure fabrication. The older brother has made it up himself. He is as cross as that. But the father does not let himself be intimidated. He says very gently, 'My son, you are always with me, and everything I have is yours. But we must feast and be happy, for your brother was dead and is now alive, he was lost and has now been found.'

So the story ends. Jesus does not go on to say whether the older brother persevered in his attitude and went off embittered, or whether he said, 'Indeed, father, you're right. It is truly amazing that my brother has come back. It's a good thing for you and a good thing for him. I've never really understood you. I've always been your slave. I always thought that you simply gave orders; I never realized that you loved me.'

The sequel is left to the hearer's imagination, as in the story of the labourers in the vineyard. Perhaps the labourers went back home in a sulk. But they may suddenly have been delighted that the others had done so little and had earned so much. They may have been pleased about a goodness which was there without having to be earned.

Was Jesus a self-seeking, authoritarian personality? Whatever one may think, he always treated his fellow-men with great respect, and did not force them in any way. What he did 'with authority' was to create a situation in which they could make their own decisions. That, too, is clear from all sorts of stories which went the rounds among the first Christians. I think that one of the most impressive of them is the story of the woman caught in adultery. The incident is sketched out in a few short strokes. The essential details are given and all the rest is left to the hearer's imagination. The scene is a forecourt of the temple. Jesus is giving instruction sitting down, as was usual for a teacher. Then scribes and Pharisees come up with a woman who has been caught in adultery. They set her in the midst and then say to Jesus, 'Master, this woman has been caught in the act of adultery. In the law, Moses commanded us to stone such women. But what do you say?' Jesus bends forward and sits there writing in the sand with his finger. They persist with their questions until he straightens up and says, 'Let him among you who is without sin cast the first stone.' Then he goes on writing on the ground. Thereupon they go away one by one, beginning with the oldest, who was probably their spokesman. When at last only the woman is left standing in front of him, Jesus says, 'Where are they? Has no one condemned you?' She replies, 'No one, sir.' Then Jesus says, 'No more do I condemn you. Go away and don't sin again.'

This story also shows how the scribes and Pharisees use their case in order to trap Jesus. By concluding that the woman should be stoned, Jesus could perhaps have been accused of disobedience to an official Roman regulation. If he let her go free, then he was not observing the law of Moses. We find similar attempts to trap him in other stories. What Jesus in fact does is to make people think. They claim that they are concerned with law and order, so they must see that wickedness is punished. They have given themselves a particular role and they have to play it. Jesus makes them well aware of that. He acts rather like a competent psychiatrist. He listens and keeps quiet, for some time. Then he reminds his questioners of their personal life, their secrets, and in so doing he makes them confused. While Jesus sits there writing quietly in the sand, they disappear from the scene one by one. Their common purpose is disrupted. It was based on their shared concern for the law to be observed. Jesus has not passed judgment one way or the other. He has simply made them think, while he has been sitting quietly and looking at the ground. This has made it possible for them to depart unobtrusively, certain that they will not feel his gaze on their backs as they go.

What Jesus was writing in the sand is left to the hearer's imagination. So is what the woman felt after her accusers had departed one by one. No decision had been made, and in the end they stood there alone. The impersonal law had vanished from sight, along with those who had required conformity to it. Now the woman had become a person instead of a 'case': Jesus was talking to her. He asked whether she too saw the situation for what it was. Then he gave his judgment. What she had done was bad, but he did not blame her or threaten her. He simply showed her that she was free. This short story also shows something of the impression which Jesus made on people. Such an approach was completely novel in their society; it had 'authority', but it was so outgoing, so concerned for the subjects. Jesus lived in the deep conviction that here too he was fulfilling 'the will of God'. In his view, this was the way in which God exercised his authority among men, not by compulsion and force, but by invitation, appealing to people to act from inner motivation and to become free so as to be able to be good towards others.

One might perhaps put it this way: Jesus believed that he had been called to make clear God's way of acting, to 'reveal' it. He devoted himself wholly to this task. It must have been in the group of twelve that he once began to speak explicitly on the theme of authority. The occasion was perhaps a conversation about which of the twelve would take over the leadership if Jesus left them, who would lord it over the others. Jesus then pointed to the way in which men were to live together in the 'kingdom of God', that is, when God was seen for who he was. 'In the forms of society which you know, there are always rulers and subjects. There are potentates and great lords, and they let the little men feel that they are in charge. But among you things must be quite different. The important man among you is the one who serves the others.' The group was never to forget how he had shown what that meant. He, the undisputed leader of their group, the one who was behind the whole enterprise, went round serving them while they sat at table. This may also have been the time when he said he would go to any lengths to teach men this completely new way of living together.

8

Why he Had to Die

We now come to the problem of Christ's suffering and death. In readings, hymns and sermons about it in church you often hear the words 'must', 'had to': everything had to happen in this way because God had decreed and ordained it. This way of speaking might give the impression that Jesus really could not avoid his terrible fate. He had never had any choice. Centuries before, God had already revealed his plan for his Messiah, his Christ. It was set out in the words of the prophets, in the holy books. No one could alter the course of events, because 'the scriptures must be fulfilled'. You can also often hear mention in church of God's 'plan of salvation'. For many centuries the almighty God, who was utterly good, had allowed evil and sin to rampage over the earth. When he thought the time had come, he sent his Son and made him die to atone for our sins. He chose his own Son as a sacrifice. By doing this he opened up a source of reconciliation for all men. Those who believe in Christ, who died on the cross for our sins, can be purified from all their sins, and be 'washed clean in his blood'.

Christians ought to have some awareness of the great objections which thoughtful and sensitive people have to this way of thinking. These objections are by no means new, but go back over a century and more. Many people feel that the belief outlined in the previous paragraph attributes an immoral action to God. Moreover, they think that it is unworthy of our humanity to shift the consequences of our wickedness on to the sole figure of Christ. However, I cannot go into that now. We have to try to get some idea of the actual course of events: how Jesus came to be executed. We are concerned with something

59

that happened here on earth, something that human beings did to one another.

There was also an element of necessity in these events. They were bound to happen. Here, however, the necessity is of a kind that does not involve God. Whenever a youth goes out in heavy traffic on his hotted-up motor bike without a crash-helmet we say, 'That's stupid, he's bound to have an accident.' Whenever an oppressive régime, a dictatorship, resorts to force in keeping order, we say, 'That's bound to lead to rebellion.' Things just turn out that way. Or to look at the second example in another light: if someone living under a harsh dictatorship openly criticizes the régime, and doesn't mince words in doing so, then one day or another he is bound to be eliminated, to be silenced by the authorities.

This second illustration brings us close to Jesus' case. It was not that he encouraged rebellion against the authorities, but he believed in God and preached about him so differently from the official religious teachers that he was bound to come into conflict with the Jewish religious leaders. At least, that would happen if he did not compromise. If he stuck to what he did, if he remained faithful to his calling as he saw it and tried to carry it out, the authorities *were bound* to silence him by force.

The Jews had no doctrinal authority of the kind that is to be found in many Christian churches. By that I mean a body concerned with whether what church members preach or write about God and man and the Bible and so on is doctrinally sound, which calls them to order if their preaching does not follow the official line. Before the destruction of Jerusalem by the Romans in AD 70, there was no fixed body of doctrine among the Jews, no 'orthodoxy'. In Jesus' time there was a great variety of opinions. In an important question like that of 'the hereafter', for example, anyone could believe what he wanted. Some Jews expected retribution after death, a resurrection and eternal life. Others expected nothing at all, and said that when a person died that was that. The latter were by no means second-class Jews.

Jews felt that the most important feature of religion was what one did and the way in which one behaved. The true believers were those who lived their lives wholly in accordance with the Torah, including all the 613 commandments and prohibitions which regulated every aspect of life. Anyone who wanted to be righteous, to be certain that he had a right relationship with his God, always had to take them into account.

The Torah dominated everything. Perhaps one should go further and say that it was an article of faith with which no Jew could tamper. The God of Israel had expressed his will in it for ever. It was a revelation of his nature which he had given to his people Israel.

The Torah was God's great act of grace to his people, the proof of Israel's election. Pious Jews could not speak about the Torah without indulging in paeans of thanks and praise. However much beliefs and expectations may have differed in the Jewish groups and parties, no one had any doubt at all about the divine character of the Torah and its decisive role in the past (even at creation!), the present and the future.

This may be the reason why Jesus was silenced so quickly and so radically. His message was that God was now addressing every Jew directly, and no longer through the Torah. God was acting now; with the appearance of Jesus a new time had begun, the definitive period of God's kingdom and the happiness that it brought.

At this point we must pause for a moment. The question here is not just a historical one; it concerns ourselves and our attitude to life. Perhaps it is best to begin by drawing a distinction. Laws, regulations, commandments govern men's social conduct, their visible actions. Laws always allow a degree of latitude. Alongside this level of social conduct, or perhaps underlying it, can be found the sphere of personal relationships. In this sector, on this level, laws, regulations or commandments count for nothing. Trust, surrender, love and their opposites come from within. A lawgiver can make no stipulations here.

I have just mentioned the latitude which laws and regulations allow. Here is a simple example. The law in Holland states that shops must close at six o'clock in the evening. Some shops may keep to the letter of the law: at six o'clock precisely the doors are shut, and after that no customers can be served. They are sent away politely but firmly: 'We have to keep to the law.' Other shops may be less fussy: customers are served provided that they are actually in the shop by six o'clock. In some cases, shopkeepers may even encourage neighbours and friends to come in just before six, so that they can go on selling until half-past six or even later and still keep 'within the law'. This phrase conjures up the picture of a particular area with a definite boundary. Anyone who goes beyond the boundary fence 'breaks' the law. Another way of putting it is to say that you do not come up against the law as long as you keep within certain limits.

There are so many laws that sometimes the ordinary citizen does not know precisely what is legal and what is not, whether he has broken the law or not. In important questions, for example where he finds himself being prosecuted, he will enlist the help of a lawyer. Our word 'advocate' comes from the Latin and means 'someone who is called in'. He is experienced enough to be able to argue in court that his client has kept within the limits; he knows all the laws and the latitude that they allow.

The Jews served God by doing his will, and God's will was laid down in the Torah, with all its commandments and prohibitions. This type of religion made a great deal of work for lawyers. They knew all the laws and regulations, and could also explain what a person could or could not do in a particular instance. They worked out, as it were, how much latitude he had. In other words, they established what people could do without coming against the boundary fence, the point at which legislation had set a limit. It goes without saying that there were great differences of opinion among the lawyers. In the time of Jesus, one group or school allowed very little latitude, and expounded the Law strictly. They were like our first set of shopkeepers: six o'clock is six o'clock and that's that. In contrast to them, another school was much more liberal in its interpretation of the Law: you need have no qualms about serving anyone who was in the shop before six o'clock, and if someone came in as the clock was striking, it was still all right to serve him as long as he was over the threshold by the time the sixth stroke had sounded. It was all right as long as he was over the threshold, so the door did not have to be shut until then . . . Within these limits a person was still 'righteous' in the sight of God, because he had not transgressed God's Law.

Jesus disagreed. For him, religion lay on the other level, that of personal relationships. God required far more than obedience to laws and attempts to discover how much latitude they allowed. Because God loves man, there is nowhere that his will does not affect them. He wants them to love him, to see things his way, utterly and without any limit, just as he loves them — and not only them but their neighbours, and even the lepers in their midst and their sworn enemies. The Law provides a basis for judging people and giving them labels and dividing them into groups: pious and sinners, clean and unclean, Jews and Gentiles. However, the time for this is now past, and so is this kind of thinking and judging and dividing into groups; now God makes a direct and personal appeal to men's hearts.

The 'conversion' or 'repentance' which Jesus required was directly concerned with this. People were to turn towards the God who loved them and who wanted to form a perfect society which would include everyone without exception and bring them closer to each other and to him. That meant devoting one's whole life to God, turning to him with all one's heart. It involved doing everything possible to bring about real friendship among people: being completely open towards others, even towards one's enemies; always being ready to forgive and to be reconciled one more time; being completely honest with everyone and keeping one's promises. Was this resistance to the authority of the Torah? It might be more accurate to say that Jesus had to speak and act as he did on the basis of his own experience of God, and that as a result he showed up the whole system as being unsatisfactory and obsolete.

That was bound to lead to conflict. There are not enough facts for us to be able to sketch out the course that it took. Perhaps Jesus first preached for a while on the basis of his own experience of God, utterly elated and confident that his joy and his devotion to God would get through to people. Then after a while he may have come up against resistance, above all from the lawyers. They will have had questions and criticisms which will have shown Jesus how much his preaching ran counter to the prevailing modes of thought. However, once again, we simply do not know how the conflict arose or what course it took.

We can see clearly from the reminiscences of the first Christians that Jesus often acted and spoke in a provocative way. Whereas the lawyers kept themselves very busy discussing all kinds of regulations about the sabbath, what people could and could not do, Jesus chose that very day for his cures. He was not at all bothered whether they were lawful or not. If a particular day is set aside for God, it is a day for doing good to people. Jesus often sat down to meals with 'unclean' people who according to the system had been excluded from God's community. He described how God cared even for them and sought them out, and whenever they listened to his invitation, he joined them in celebrating the overwhelming goodness of his God.

We need to be aware just how preoccupied the pious Jews were with not touching or eating or drinking anything unclean, if we are to understand the impact that some of Jesus' sayings would make: 'Nothing coming from outside can make a man unclean; only what comes from his heart.' Remember how pious Jews had undergone torture and death for refusing to eat anything unclean!

Here is another example of his provocative way of speaking. Perhaps in answer to a question he was asked about divorce (a burning question even in those days), he remarked: 'Anyone who puts away his wife makes her commit adultery, and anyone who marries such a woman also commits adultery.'

To understand just how remarkable this comment was and how challenging it must have seemed, we need first of all to know something about the position of women in Jewish society. In a prayer used by pious Jews at the time of Jesus, we can read the words: 'Praised be God that he did not make me a Gentile. Praised be God that he did not make me a woman. Praised be God that he did not make me a fool.' That was the status accorded to women: they were in the same class as Gentiles and fools. They were also 'fools' in that they did not and could not know anything about the Torah. They were not allowed to concern themselves with it, nor might they be instructed in it.

64

To know the will of God and to busy oneself with it was the exclusive prerogative of men.

A married woman, too, was completely without rights. Her husband could put her away whenever he wanted. He did not have to go before a judge. His only legal obligation was to write a declaration that he no longer regarded the woman he had married as his wife; when he had written this letter of separation, or divorce, he could send her away.

This regulation was based on a ruling in the Torah. The word of God was not in fact completely clear. It was said that a man could put his wife away if 'something unseemly is found in her'. Thus the Law allowed a good deal of latitude. What did this word 'unseemly' mean? I have already mentioned the two schools of lawyers in Jesus' time: those who were strict and those who were more liberal. In this instance, those who belonged to the stricter school said that by 'unseemly' God meant something very bad, a real crime, adultery. No, said the representatives of the more liberal school, 'unseemly' behaviour can simply mean that the woman allowed some food to burn, or even that the husband had found another woman more attractive.

The Torah regarded a wife as one of her husband's possessions. The tenth commandment mentions her alongside his other possessions; his house, his slaves and his cattle. So according to the word of God the husband was his wife's master, her 'owner'. Where a husband is concerned, the Torah always refers to marriage using a verb which really means, 'become master, owner of'. Hence it was in fact impossible for a husband to commit adultery. If he committed adultery with a married woman, this was simply a breach of her husband's marriage, in other words, he was violating her husband's property.

As a result, the Torah was of little use to a woman, though the 'letter of divorce' which it required was certainly intended as protection for her. It gave her tangible proof that she was 'free' and could be married again. A second marriage was usually a bitter necessity: an unmarried woman had hardly any possibility of survival in Jewish society. The requirement of a letter of divorce corresponds to requirements in the Law about

65

slaves, which were also intended as protection.

So the divine Torah gave the husband the right to get rid of his wife whenever he wanted to. Fortunately many Jews also had consciences and felt that this was inhuman. I have already mentioned the lawyers who limited the 'unseemliness' to a serious crime on the wife's part. In the time of Jesus they also tried to introduce rules which made it difficult financially for a man to get rid of his wife.

Jesus went a good deal further. He rejected divorce radically. He condemned as great wickedness, adultery, what every Jewish husband was allowed to do according to the Torah, and thus according to God himself. Moreover, he gave his own judgment the form of a divine law. The Torah often says, 'Anyone who does this or that makes himself guilty of such and such a thing.'

He also makes the husband responsible for the wickedness which he in fact forces upon his wife. 'Anyone who gets rid of his wife makes her commit adultery . . .' Her second marriage is sinful because it is an infringement of the marriage with her first husband, her first marriage.

On the subject of responsibilities towards women, it is worth noting something else that the disciples remembered. Jesus cured women as well as men; he proclaimed his message to them too, and he even included women in his company. With all this in mind, we can have some idea of how radical and provocative his remarks on divorce would seem.

It was really at this point that he set his own judgment alongside the Torah. He did this elsewhere too. According to the Torah, people were not to swear falsely and they had to honour their oaths. 'But I say to you, do not swear at all.' And on all these issues Jesus never argued, never appealed to his own authority. He simply put forward his own views. His attitude to the unclean and the sinners, and to other utterly worthless and insignificant people, such as women and even children, was also considered incredible and irresponsible. (How could he say, 'You must become like a child' – a creature which could only accept help from others and was incapable of achieving anything by itself – what nonsense!) No, Jesus' so-called teaching and the way in which he behaved seemed totally without foundation. It was incomprehensible, without any basis in revelation or tradition.

All this made Jesus insufferable. We human beings need to place someone, to classify him in some way. Otherwise he remains alien and menacing. It was impossible to classify Jesus. He did not belong to any group, and no label seemed to fit him. He gave religious teaching, like a rabbi, but he was not trained and he did not keep to the rules. He required people to repent, like a prophet, but he never spoke in the name of God ('Thus says Yahweh . . .'), and he never referred to a divine calling. Was he perhaps a second John? No, certainly not, because John led a very sober existence in the wilderness, while Jesus loved parties.

Nor could Jesus be included in one of the many factions and groups. As he himself said, he was looking for 'the lost sheep of the house of Israel', in order to bring them together again. For him, all the Jews were lost sheep: the lost figures who made up the people of Israel, particularly because they were so hopelessly divided into so many factions and groups and lonely individuals. This did not fulfil the purpose of God, who wanted to be the Father of them all. Jesus wanted to reach everyone, which is why he did not join any faction. Nor did he form a group of his own, in Essene style. You could only join their group if you obeyed certain conditions, and then you had to live according to particular rules. The group of twelve were co-workers with Jesus, but anyone who wanted to could join them.

At first sight, a visitor from abroad might have classed Jesus as a Pharisee, one of those particularly religious laymen who were keen to see the will of God done here and now by as many people as possible. But the visitor would also have noted that this very group put up the most vigorous protest against Jesus' ideas and attitudes. Many of the parables and sayings contained in the earliest evidence were told to Pharisees. He also had some harsh words to say and some bitter accusations to make to them. 'Woe to you Pharisees, whited sepulchres! You are attractive on the outside and rotten inside.' No one likes to hear that sort of thing. But sometimes you have to be harsh on those you love; perhaps this is the only way of reaching their real selves, of breaking through the thick crust of prejudice.

Still, however hard Jesus tried, even with the Pharisees, resistance steadily grew stronger. When he went up to Jerusalem towards Passover time he must have known what awaited him. He had had little to do with the priests and the higher authorities in Jerusalem. Perhaps he had attracted their attention by appearing in the Temple, where he stormed against the moneychangers and the merchants. The Temple was the priests' domain. What went on in the forecourts was not Jesus' affair. Besides, the Roman soldiers kept a lookout on the Temple precincts from their citadel, and were likely to make a blood bath there at the least provocation. And at Passover time Jerusalem was a powder keg with its thousands of pilgrims, and above all the violently anti-Roman Galileans.

It is impossible to tell precisely when Jesus acted against the merchants in the Temple and how it came about. But he will certainly have attracted the attention of the Jerusalem authorities when he fearlessly summoned people to repent even there, reminding them of God's imminent rule. The authorities were the Jewish council in Jerusalem, the supreme court (Sanhedrin). It was presided over by the high priest, and consisted mostly of Sadducees, but there were also scribes from among the Pharisees. The Sanhedrin doubtless discussed Jesus, that impossible man who was so dangerous for Israel. In one of these moods, the common people might see him as a political liberator, a 'Messiah'. That would cause an uproar, the beginning of a general rebellion; the Romans would inevitably stamp down hard on it and that might mean the end of the nation. All this was clear to the politically conscious members of the Sanhedrin. At the same time, however, the Pharisees were convinced that Jesus was undermining the spiritual foundations of the nation. He was doing so in theory, by failing to recognize the Torah as the definitive revelation of God, and even more in practice, by disregarding the laws of purity and debasing the sabbath, thus inciting people to disobedience towards God.

Jesus knew very well that his appearance in Jerusalem would lead to his death, but he went through with it. Perhaps he too felt that he was 'bound to'. He had so often said that the new reality of God's rule could demand that a man should give everything, his family, his possessions, even his life. Indeed, real life began when you could lose it. Jesus had often spoken about the way people should behave towards their enemies – even enemies were fellow human beings who were also loved by God – and about how to respond to violence: it had to be endured. Did he not have to show that he meant what he said, and live out his message?

That his message had not been just a matter of words. The life-giving power of the kingdom had been at work in his person: he had cured cripples and sick people and had brought a welcome to the outcast. God had begun to rule through Jesus, and he would continue his work of bringing all men together, in spite of the death of Jesus and indeed perhaps even through it. Who knows what compulsion Jesus may have felt towards that end?

When he was sitting at table with his twelve disciples just before his death, Jesus performed an action with the bread and wine which they were never to forget. He shared out the bread among them and said, 'This is I myself, my whole existence, devoted to God and therefore to you and to all men.' Then he passed the cup of wine round with a similar remark, 'This is my life, emptied out completely because of my Father's desire to bring you all happiness in a new covenant.'

He performed them just in time, these actions which he chose to embody himself and all that made up his life. After that there was nothing more he could do. His hands were tied. The police who arrested him brought him before the Sanhedrin. There he was tried. We know nothing for certain about the trial, but the account which says that he kept silent seems to be the earliest. The question of his authority may well have been at issue, in fact the old request for 'a sign', some authorization, some justification. In that case we can understand why Jesus kept silent. How can a man account for what his heart tells him?

The Sanhedrin sent him to Pilate. The case was not a difficult one for the governor. Jesus had aroused 'messianic' expectations, and thus instigated a rebellion against the Roman authorities. A large number of Jews had already been crucified for this, and it was only right to execute someone who seemed to be another of them just before their Passover. But this Jesus was also guilty in the eyes of the Jewish authorities: he had instigated rebellion against God himself.

— 9 —

How 'the Church' Began

Jesus did not form any party nor did he set up any organization. He had not made any arrangements for that when he died.

The Roman Catholic church tells another story. It goes something like this. Before his death Jesus, usually referred to as the Lord Christ or the Son of God, the God-man, appointed his disciple Peter head of the church, or of the community that he intended to found. He gave Peter all necessary authority in the belief that the community would last for ever. After his resurrection, Jesus completed the organization of the church: to mention one important point, he instituted the seven sacraments before he left this earth.

However, the earliest evidence gives no indication that Jesus set up any organization like a church. He wanted to bring all Jews together in a new personal relationship to God like his own, to make them into a kind of divine family. All the divisions into groups and factions which were so marked, the differences and even conflicts between them, would now vanish away. He did not form a separate group like the Pharisees, much less like the Essenes. Which raises the question: since Jesus himself did not organize or 'found' anything like a church, how did it come into being?

The question can be answered very briefly indeed. The 'church' arose out of the belief that Jesus was alive again after his death. That is the basis of its existence. However, this short answer also raises a new question: how did that belief arise?

The oldest answers to the question were, 'He has appeared to us! He has come back to us! We have seen him!' The exclamation marks have to be there, because these were not detached assertions. They were cries and shouts of joy, provoked by an unexpected reunion. It is obvious that the disciples were utterly amazed and bewildered at the 'appearance' of Jesus, and so deeply moved that they found it impossible to talk about their experience in a matter-of-fact way. We shall probably never know what form the reunions took. The stories about them preserved in our four gospels were written much later, and are certainly not meant to be read as objective accounts.

Anyone who tries to arrange them in a particular order will soon find that out. The details of people, times and places are all contradictory. However, we can discover one or two things.

First, the oldest elements in the stories point to Galilee. This implies that after Jesus' death the disciples returned to their homes, to the area from which Jesus had also come. Perhaps they fled from Jerusalem in panic immediately after the crucifixion. In any case, they had been shattered. They had never expected such an end. God had not saved Jesus from death. The Sanhedrin had been right, and Jesus had been quite wrong. It was unbelievable! Did that mean that Jesus' trust in his father, Abba, had also been an illusion? They also had the disturbing feeling that they themselves, his own disciples, had left him in the lurch. That was cowardly of them, even if Jesus had been wrong.

Secondly, despite the differences, the accounts of the appearances do have one or two things in common. Jesus always arrives suddenly, appearing unexpectedly out of nowhere. The men and women, his friends, to whom he comes, at first fail to recognize him. They sound surprised, terrified. Jesus makes a move to reveal himself to them, showing them by a word or a gesture that he is indeed the Jesus with whom they had been in such close contact. Now he is recognized. He usually asks those whom he meets to do something, sends them to others. Then once again he disappears into nowhere.

Another reaction to the appearances was: 'God has raised him!', again with an exclamation mark. Jesus proved to be alive, and that meant that the God of Israel had not abandoned him. The Jewish authorities had condemned him as a 'blasphemer' and therefore had excommunicated him. But this same God had raised him to life. So the authorities were wrong, and not Jesus. This meant that the way in which he had dealt with the Torah had been the right way. God was on his side, and therefore stood behind all that he had said and done. So God really was as Jesus had experienced him and proclaimed him: he was in search of his people because he loved them, whoever they might be and however far they might have strayed from him. God writes no one off, he is just like the father of the prodigal son. He has enormous respect for his people's freedom, as Jesus had shown. So what he does is to make people ask questions about themselves, think about their lives, always drawing them on and sometimes offending them in order to break down the hard crust in which they are encased. He does all this because he loves men and is concerned for them; he is insistent, but never forces anyone against their will.

'Jesus lives!' also means that he remains active, or rather, that he now goes on with his work in an even more intensive way. This conviction was also expressed in the stories about his 'appearances'. He continually arrives from nowhere and then vanishes again. That means that he has been taken up into the unimaginable fullness of life and love which are denoted by the word 'God'. He 'appears' from there, seeks contact with his disciples and 'sends' them. Jesus lives with God, but not for himself; he continues in a new way what he began in his life on earth: his urgent invitation to everyone to be open to his God and to discover one another in this new openness, to find happiness as instruments of his activity, to bring together in his name men who will live for God and for one another. The first witnesses to Jesus' resurrection were full of this fact, so they formed a 'church', a group to which they belonged as a base from which to go out to others.

The first members of the church began to do this very quickly. Now they experienced personally something of the remarkable authority of Jesus, his utter confidence in the God for whom no man is too unimportant, and they acted in the strength which he had communicated and with his courage. No power in the world could cause them any anxiety. Certainly not the Roman rulers, much less the Jewish Sanhedrin. Both authorities had thought that they could do away with Jesus. They had failed.

The strength which Jesus communicated proved effective and also affected others. The new belief spread like a forest fire. The followers of Jesus formed groups in an increasing number of cities. So there began the phenomenon which is described in the history books as 'the rapid expansion of Christianity'.

We Catholics used to learn that this rapid expansion was manifestly a divine miracle, a proof that Christian belief is 'true' and really comes from God, just as the miracles prove the divinity of Jesus. Such an argument no longer works in our time, but even if we no longer regard the success of the Jesus movement in the early days as a miracle, it remains a striking phenomenon, and historians will always be preoccupied with it. We have discussed all this earlier: again and again new facts emerge to colour their views.

One point from this period of history is also important for us here. The question arose who Jesus was, or rather, who he became in relation to his fellow men. That includes what he meant after his death to those who were so to speak caught up in the first explosion of the new way of living. We have already seen that Palestine was by no means a backward country. It had connections with the great cities of the Roman empire. People travelled a good deal in the countries around the Mediterranean, particularly when the great emperor Augustus had succeeded, shortly before the birth of Jesus, in bringing peace almost everywhere, and with it a degree of security and indeed prosperity. Ease of travel meant that there could be a close network of communication among the Jews, who had a synagogue in every city of any importance. The nucleus of each community was formed by Jews who were descended from the old tribe of Judah, which is why they were given the name 'Jew'. They were often joined by proselytes. These were people from the Gentile world who had accepted the faith, or rather, had been accepted into 'the Jewish people': they were so to speak 'naturalized' Jews. They had taken upon themselves to fulfil all the regulations of the Torah and all the Jewish customs.

On the periphery there was often a large group of 'God-fearers'. These too were Gentiles who felt attracted to the Jewish faith, but who did not want to go so far as to take all the requirements of the Torah upon themselves. Even though the Jews in the great cities of the empire did not fulfil these requirements as scrupulously as the strict Pharisees in Palestine, it was a heavy burden.

Judaism was especially attractive because of its recognition of only one God, the creator and king of all; Jews therefore proudly rejected the plethora of pagan gods and goddesses with their immoral adventures. Moreover, the Jews had a clear view of the world and its meaning and purpose. Above all, their way of life and their morality, not least their sense of the family, corresponded to their exalted belief in God. Other 'eastern' deities were also popular in Graeco-Roman cities, but for many people they did not have the attraction of Judaism.

However, admiration for synagogue worship and even participation in it was rather different from being a proselyte. To become a 'naturalized' Jew presented problems. It meant being circumcised, which was painful as well as barbarous. Observing the sabbath involved abnormal behaviour. Then there was the burden of obeying all the regulations about purity, which were particularly troublesome when it came to eating and drinking. This kind of faith and life-style isolated one from society; it asked too much.

Then the story of Jesus came out of Palestine. Its implications were amazing. The God of the Jews had now broken down the barriers himself. That was the significance of the message of Jesus and his story. The one God, the creator and king, had now revealed his deepest feelings: he loved every human being just as they were, no matter what their past. This was what Jesus had preached and how he had lived. This was why he was rejected by the guardians of the Torah. But God had proved him right, and therefore had written off the whole system of living and thinking and judging in accordance with the Torah. He wanted to have a deeper relationship with people.

That was the end! The end of the world as it had been hitherto, and the beginning of a completely new world, the world as it should be. That was also the significance of the resurrection of Jesus to a new life in God. He was the first of a new humanity, for whom there was to be no more anxiety, because nothing mattered at all, not even death. The followers of Jesus gave some indication of that new life by their unprecedented openness, their discovery of one another, their freedom from all the prejudices that had previously kept them apart or set them at variance.

On the whole, whenever those who proclaimed the new message arrived in a particular city, they went first to the synagogue. Of course the Jews there found their story difficult to take. It was impossible that someone who had transgressed the Torah, who had been condemned by the Sanhedrin and tried by the Romans, could be a man of God, indeed *the* man, the Messiah. Those who proclaimed the message might point to all kinds of passages in scripture, but these passages did not say what they were thought to mean. This was hardly an exposition of scripture; it was sheer invention. You could prove anything that way! However, the message made an immediate impact on many God-fearers. On the whole these were the ones who formed the nucleus of a new Jesus community in the cities. They were less isolated than the Jews and the proselytes, and quickly passed on their story to friends and acquaintances who knew virtually nothing about Judaism.

We should not forget that in the chief cities of the Roman empire there were countless people who really had no firm basis for religious belief. The old religions were inadequate; at a much earlier time they had had close links with social and economic groups in particular areas. Since then things had changed completely, especially after the conquests of Alexander the Great and the establishment of his empire. Now, in the time of Caesar Augustus, 'classical' religion was over and done with. Hence the interest in all kinds of religions from the East. Many people also sought security in mysteries like magic and astrology. For despite a certain degree of external prosperity, the dominant feeling was one of pessimism, of utter defeatism. People felt that they were in the hands of powers against which they could do nothing. There was not only the political power of the Romans, there were above all the mysterious powers of the universe, the planets and the stars: the course of one's life was determined in these heavenly regions. How could a man affect that? This kind of question dominated the spiritual atmosphere, even where it was not put in so many words.

Countless people were swallowed up into the great cities, isolated among the masses. 'Such loneliness must have been felt by millions: the urbanised tribesman, the peasant come to town in search of work, the demobilised soldier, the rentier ruined by inflation and the manumitted slave': so the situation was summed up by a great modern scholar. He concluded: 'For people in that situation membership of a Christian community might be the only way of maintaining self-respect and giving their life some semblence of meaning. Within the community there was human warmth: someone was interested in them, both here and here-after. It is therefore not surprising that the earliest and most striking advances of Christianity were made in the great cities — in Antioch, in Rome, in Alexandria.'

The people who responded to the story of Jesus, the almost incredible news of the one God who cared for everyone, came together and formed a group, a 'church'. Then they went on to form other groups. Groups which formed in the great cities became as it were centres from which members passed on their liberating news to those who lived in the small towns and villages around. Spreading the good news was an integral part of the story of Jesus. It was not something that you could keep to yourself; you had to pass it on and involve others in it. That is what the 'church' is: a group around Jesus, which above all is open to others.

When people met together on 'the Lord's day', the day of Jesus' resurrection from the dead, our 'Sunday', there was a great deal of excitement. Don't forget that we are talking about the countries around the Mediterranean Sea, where people express their feelings much more readily than we northerners do. When they recalled Jesus and the God whom he made so real, they became ecstatic, and in this state they uttered in-comprehensible sounds: speaking in tongues. There was singing and rejoicing, but also a good deal of talk and discussion. There had to be. The Christians shared a particular experience and they had to work out what it was. Because it was completely new, there were as yet no accepted terms with which to describe it. Nor was there any one authority. Each member of the community could make his or her own contribution. And there was a good deal to talk about in connection with the person of Jesus, his death and resurrection, the new relationship with God, the new future for men and for the world.

Now there was in fact one established terminology for discussing God, man and the world. It was to be found in the ancient book of the Jews, which had been translated into Greek a century or so earlier, and was used in the synagogues. The first members of a Jesus group always included people who knew the scriptures well. Moreover, the way in which the story of Jesus was handed down already had a biblical colouring. However, in the new situation which the God of Israel had created, many of the old words were inevitably given a new content. The Jesus groups were often involved in this. What happened differed from place to place, so the writings in our New Testament are often very difficult to understand. One needs not only to have a good knowledge of the Old Testament, but also to understand the different ways in which the various passages were interpreted in the Jewish centres of the Roman empire. Study of the background to the New Testament steadily continues, and is never likely to come to an end. Hundreds of scholars throughout the world are regularly engaged in it.

I would like to spend a little more time on one term from the Old Testament, the reference book of the early Christians. This is the word 'spirit', or 'the Holy Spirit'. The first Christians tended to use the term in connection with the way in which Jesus came alive to them and worked among them. That is precisely the point that concerns us here. The word 'spirit' was also used frequently in the language of the church, and many people are often uncertain what it means. So if we look back, perhaps we may be able to get a better idea of what the first Christians thought and felt whenever they talked about 'the Holy Spirit'.

The Greek word for spirit really means blowing, wind, breeze, and also breath, that gentle current of air which indicates that someone is still animated, alive. We find the same thing in Jewish scripture. Wherever we come across the word 'spirit' in an English Old Testament, it is a translation of the Hebrew word which also means 'wind' or 'blowing'. It can also denote a strong wind, a hurricane, as well as a breeze, and, of course, breath. Whenever the wind blows up into a storm, it can break large trees like matchsticks. It is a powerful force, but you cannot see it. So it is a sign of the mysterious activity of God; you can see his work, but you cannot see God himself. Breath is just as miraculous. The ancient Israelites spoke of 'the breath of life', indeed, breath *is* the life that God has breathed into men. Thus every man in fact lives by the breath of God. But in ancient times it might also happen that an ordinary man suddenly performed a mighty act in order to free Israel. A commonplace farmer would all at once become a leader and a hero. When that happened, people said that the storm-wind or the breath of God had come upon him and had made a new man of him. In other words, God had blown over him with great force and breathed new life into him. In our translations it is said that 'the spirit of the Lord came upon him'.

In later centuries, when devout Jews suffered because their community was weak and divided, and so many of their number were slack or in despair, a prophet would address them in this way: 'People, a time is coming when our God will breathe on you again, when new life will blaze up, and then we shall all be full of him, young and old, high and low, men and women, masters and slaves. Then he will make us all new men.'

'That is just how we feel,' said the first Christians, or rather, they shouted it out aloud. 'God has never before breathed his life into men as he has done now. He has gone back to creating again. We have become new men in a completely new community. Whatever we were beforehand, whatever group we used to belong to, Jews, Greeks, barbarians, free citizens, slaves, men, women, old or young, God has breathed deeply on us from above and this has made us find one another.'

That is why there was so much talk about the Spirit of God or the Holy Spirit during this first period. The members of the movement could see tempestuous things happening in and through people: new attitudes and new relationships were developing. So instead of saying, 'God is at work here', they preferred to use the Old Testament expression: the breath or the wind of God, the Holy Spirit, is at work.

But it all had to do with Jesus. It came about as a result of what had happened: his appearance and what God had done through him. God had brought him to life, had in fact created this dead man anew; that, too, was the work of his breath of life, his Spirit. And the result was that the power of Jesus had gone to work in a much more intensive way than before: wherever his message was proclaimed, this power seemed to seize people, to make them open to God and to each other, and to involve them in a whole new series of attitudes and relationships and expectations.

We have just been speaking of the power which went out from Jesus. In most contexts, we may perhaps best think of the blowing, the breath, the wind that we know by this word 'Spirit', or 'Holy Spirit', in terms of a magnetic force or field of force. But we should not think of it as impersonal energy; rather, it is an appeal which affects people, involves them, catches hold of them, and that means that it is itself personal.

Here we come up against an ambiguity in the writing of the first Christians. Sometimes that personal power, the Holy Spirit, seems to come from Jesus himself. In other words, Christians feel themselves involved and caught up with Jesus himself. So one of them can write: 'the Lord Jesus *is* the Spirit'. But often the power which emanates from Jesus, the personal appeal, the Holy Spirit, is distinguished from him. In that case the texts say that Jesus 'sends his Spirit'. Here is an illustration, chosen quite arbitrarily.

The last book of the Bible, Revelation or the Apocalypse, was written by a man called John who had been arrested by the Roman authorities and had been put in a prison camp on the small island of Patmos in the Mediterranean. This happened towards the year AD 100. John was a leader, in charge of the Jesus groups in a number of places: Ephesus, Smyrna, Pergamum and other provincial cities in Asia Minor. It is probable that the

Romans insisted that the emperor should be worshipped there as Kyrios, the lord of all men. The Christians refused. Jesus was the only Lord of all. The Romans did what they always do with resistance movements: they tried to eliminate the leaders. That is why John found himself in a concentration camp on Patmos, far from the Jesus groups which he had led, his 'seven churches'.

Perhaps they kept their banished leader in touch with what was happening in the communities and how they were coping with the measures imposed by the Roman authorities and all kinds of other difficulties. Be that as it may, they were very much in John's mind, especially on Sundays, when he knew that they were meeting together to celebrate the meal instituted by Jesus, in which he came to them again when they re-enacted what he had done with the bread and the wine. On one such Sunday, John himself was again overwhelmed by the reality of Jesus. At least, this is what he tells us at the beginning of his remarkable book. He was taken out of himself, and in this state he heard a voice behind him. He looked round, and saw the figure of Jesus, a blinding light, so overwhelming that he fell to the ground. Then Jesus touched him and said, 'Do not be afraid, it is I, the first and the last. I was dead, and look, I am alive for ever. And I have the keys of the kingdom of the dead.'

You can see from this whole description how a Christian of those first days filled out the new experience, the belief that 'Jesus lives with God'. John writes that the glorious figure is like a Son of man: he has a golden girdle round his loins, his head and hair are like snow-white wool, his feet are like bronze and his voice sounds like the rushing of mighty waters . . . All these comparisons are taken from passages in the books of Ezekiel and Daniel, in which these men tried to give some idea of their experience of the presence of God.

Jesus then says to John that he is 'the first and the last'. The book of Isaiah makes God say this of himself: he is the origin and the goal of all creation. In other words, he is the ruler of history, of everything that happens in the world from beginning to end. So, Jesus has a share in this divine activity. But what he goes on to say cannot have been taken from the

Old Testament. For this is what happened *to the man* Jesus: 'I was dead, and behold, I live for evermore.' The consequences of this unprecedented, utterly new situation are then expressed in an image used by conquerors. When a conqueror captured a city, a country, an empire, he took over the keys from the former ruler: 'And I have the keys of death and the kingdom of the dead.' Now that Jesus is with God, death has no more power. Jesus has conquered it.

The conqueror of death is actively at work among his people. This belief is expressed by John in his vision of the glorified Son of man between seven golden candlesticks: these are the Jesus communities, the churches, in the seven cities. He now addresses a letter to each of the seven churches in the name of the Son of man. He seems to know precisely what each of the groups has to endure and at what points they need to be admonished and strengthened in their hopes and expectations. Each letter ends with a promise to 'him who is victorious'. And in each case the conclusion is the same: 'Hear, you that have ears to hear, what the Spirit says to the churches.'

So we have the remarkable fact that it is really John, the leader of the churches, who is writing here. He feels that he is a 'prophet' of Jesus, and that Jesus is addressing the communities through him. At the same time, it is the Spirit which is speaking at the deepest level to the churches. The summons Jesus gave as he went round Palestine, asking men to turn to God in a completely new way in the assurance that they would have a new life, is now repeated to people in these cities. As they hear it and respond to it, they begin to discover one another in it. Their leader has become a man who has been grasped by the new reality in a quite special way and who has the gift of being able to express it. So it is through him that Jesus' invitation and promises come alive to the communities. These promises are all the more evocative in that they now come from the island of Patmos, to which John has been banished, as he himself says in his writing, 'because of the word of God and the testimony to Jesus'. He too, then, shares in the fate of Jesus.

By way of example, let me quote the conclusion of the seventh letter. John addresses the community which he feels to be really lacking in spirit: the people of Jesus in Laodicea are neither hot nor cold. One has the impression from the letter that John feels that they are having too comfortable a life. After one or two allusions to the riches and the various industries of the city, the letter ends like this: 'Be on your mettle and repent. Here I stand knocking at the door: if anyone hears my voice and opens the door, I will come in and sit down to supper with him, and he with me. To him who is victorious I will grant a place on my throne, as I myself was victorious and sat down with my Father on his throne. Hear, you who have ears to hear, what the Spirit says to the churches!'

In this passage the words of 'the Spirit' seem to correspond to the words of Jesus, and it is in fact John who is speaking. To put things less formally: a Christian is talking to others about his concern and his words are regarded as the words of Jesus and at the same time as the words of 'the Spirit'.

In another New Testament book, the Fourth Gospel, 'the Spirit' seems to be distinguished clearly from Jesus himself. The writer of the gospel was also called John, but it is open to question whether this John is the same as the one who was put in the concentration camp on Patmos.

The gospel was written about sixty years after Jesus' death in a city outside Palestine where people spoke and thought in Greek. The members of the Jesus group had to cope with critical questions from outsiders which they had also had to ask themselves. Sixty years before, a man called Jesus had travelled around the distant and unruly land of Palestine, and ultimately had been crucified by Pilate. Christians now claimed that this man had given visible expression to the ultimate realities, he was the 'revelation' of God. For a Greek that was very difficult to imagine. How could the eternal, what was true everywhere and for all time, have been made visible in a mortal, one of the millions of human beings who are born, live out their lives and then die? Greeks associated the word 'divine' with those things that are above our temporary and transitory state, with the true and good and beautiful at all times and in all places. How could that have been fully revealed in one individual from among the countless men who have ever lived? The Christian reply was: 'You have to have shared in that life and that death to see that it could indeed have been.' But such an appeal was to impossible evidence. God, or at least the 'revelation' of the divine, was being fixed to a piece of the past that was irrevocably past.

Perhaps Christians who were addressed in this way just looked helplessly at one another. They themselves knew that it was indeed possible to have new life, life full of hope, on the basis of that piece of the past. Precisely that had given a completely new turn to their lives. But how were you to explain it to someone who had not had the experience? Perhaps they said to one another, 'How can you explain what red looks like to anyone who has been born blind, or the difference between green and blue? It is impossible to explain to anyone who cannot see. You would have to give him sight, and you cannot.' They probably used another example: how can you explain what love is to anyone who has never experienced it? The reason why I suggest this is that we also have a couple of letters from the John who wrote the Fourth Gospel. In the first of them we read, 'Anyone who does not love, does not know God, for God is love.' If you limit yourself to talk *about* the divine or *about* revelation or *about* the past, you will never get anywhere; or rather, you will never find yourself in the world where Christian belief is at home. That is where men love one another.

The writer of the Fourth Gospel often makes his Jesus talk about himself as the one who reveals God, his 'Father': 'I am the truth; I am the life; I and the Father are one. Whoever sees me sees the Father.' But he also makes Jesus explain why it is unnecessary to have been with him, as the one who reveals God. He makes Jesus promise, shortly before his death, that he will send someone else, the Spirit or the Helper. The Spirit will not go away again, and will remain with the disciples for ever. He will constantly remind them of what Jesus said and did, and will make clear to them the deepest meaning of these events. 'It is good for you that I should go away. If I do not go, then the Helper will not come among you. But if I do go, I will send him to you.'

At first sight, the Spirit seems to be someone different here. But his role will be simply to maintain the relationship between Jesus and later believers. So he adds nothing to what has already been given through Jesus. Or rather, he demonstrates and explains what this means for believers in countless new situations.

The writer of the Fourth Gospel must have meditated endlessly on that basic fact: the 'historical' life of Jesus is a bit of the past beyond recall, yet it is still constantly at work, and affects men in their deepest relationships, in 'love'. This is the foundation of Christianity. 'We experience this happening and believe that in it we can see the work of God, his creative breath, his Spirit.'

The evangelist depicts what we have just referred to in the twofold scene with which he ends his gospel. He has Jesus appearing after his death to his twelve disciples, who are together in a closed room, 'on the first day of the week'. The Christians gave this name to Sunday, the day on which they regularly celebrated the coming of their Lord. Jesus' greeting also sounds liturgical: 'Peace be with you.' He shows them his wounds. The disciples recognize him with joy. Then he breathes on them and says, 'Receive the Holy Spirit.' It is a commission. Now they can hand on Jesus' power.

But the writer has his later readers in mind, so he tells how one of the Twelve was absent from this meeting, and attributes to him a critical remark which was to be heard down the ages: 'I shall only believe if I have seen and touched him myself.' Then he describes Jesus' appearing again the next Sunday. Thomas may now see and touch as much as he wants. But he simply exclaims, 'My Lord and my God!' What Jesus says after this is his last remark in this profound gospel. The writer, or rather the poet, the composer, has earlier been 'playing' with the theme of seeing and believing. You can be with Jesus, look with your eyes, like the Jews, and in fact fail to see who he really was. You only see that when you believe, i.e. accept him as the God whom you address through him. But for that you do not need to have seen him with your own eyes. That is unnecessary, and clearly does not guarantee anything. As the example of Thomas shows, you do not have to have been present yourself.

The story is enough. Those who tell it are completely trust-worthy: Jesus himself has breathed on them. Hence Jesus' last remark: 'Blessed are (he means, all is well with) those who have not seen with their own eyes and yet have believed.'

⟞ 10 ⟝

Complications Again

Jesus made religion, the service of God, very simple indeed. Now the ordinary man could also take part in it. He no longer had to know all the commandments and the prohibitions in order to be 'righteous', i.e. to live in a right relationship with God. Nor did he need any lawyers to explain to him what he could and what he could not do.

Jesus said something like this: 'Do to your neighbour what you would want him to do to you. Then you will all be happy and consequently do precisely what God wants you to do, precisely what he instructed you to do in the Law and the prophets, all these books and their interpretations, which they have made into such a complicated system of divine revelation.'

Most people know the saying, 'Do not do to anyone else what you would not want to have done to you.' In this form, which says what you must *not* do, the saying is very old. It can be found in China centuries before Christ, and it was also known among the Jews. But the *positive* form in which Jesus gives the saying, 'Do to others what you hope and expect that they would do to you,' has yet to be discovered in writings before his time, which makes it seem quite probable that he is responsible for it. For Jesus, then, this is the only way of serving God, this is the only true religion. Nothing can be simpler than that.

Remember that the Jews who were really religious devoted a great deal of time to the study of the Torah. I have already mentioned the archaeological excavations by the Dead Sea, where I saw the Essene scriptorium being brought to light. Their life was dominated by their zeal for God, which is why they studied the Torah so incessantly. From the rules of their community we can see how they felt it necessary for someone to be at work with God's word all the time, even at night. Catholics might be reminded of a constant devotional watch before the reserved sacrament.

That is no longer necessary, said Jesus, now that God himself has become active among us and addresses himself to everyone. Give up your selfish attitudes and think what you would really like from the people around you: help when you are in need comfort when you are lonely, concern, care, and love. Then treat the people you meet in the same way. Or better, see to people's needs at any particular time, give them what you yourself would want in their situation. If you do that regularly, then you will have done what God once revealed as his will in the Law and the prophets; you will be serving God.

The ordinary man, who did not know the Law, and therefore was officially 'a sinner', was really more open to God than the man who was well versed in the Torah. So Jesus seemed to think. The sinner seemed less reluctant to heed God's call. Jesus' story about the good Samaritan points in this direction. The man on his way from Jerusalem to Jericho who was attacked by robbers and left half-dead by the roadside had been noticed first by the priest who came along and later by the levite. But both of them went past. Jesus does not tell us why; the hearer is left to fill in the details himself. My explanation would be that the two men were utterly obsessed with God and his Torah, the most important things they could conceive of. Moreover, the badly-wounded man could well have been unclean. If he died on their hands, he certainly would have been; in that case they would have touched a corpse. This would have made them unclean according to the Law; they would no longer be able to approach God and would be unfit to serve as priest or levite for a while. That was bad, quite apart from its financial consequences.

Then a Samaritan came along. He, too, saw the badly wounded man lying there and, says Jesus, was moved with compassion; he did everything possible for him. To any of Jesus' hearers, a Samaritan was someone whose religious practice was quite outside the pale; he was worse than a sinner who had regularly broken the Law, and worse than a Gentile. One could put it even more strongly: he was an arch-enemy of God and his Torah. Jesus did not have to spell this out; it was implied in the name Samaritan, which was also used as a term of abuse — as if we were to say 'dirty atheist'. Now why does Jesus introduce a Samaritan like this as the person who immediately does something about a man in trouble after the priest and the levite have passed him by? We are left to fill in the details for ourselves. It seems to me that Jesus chooses someone who is not so obsessed with God and his Torah that he has no heart: he can still be just a fellow human being, deeply moved by another's suffering.

Jesus, then, believed and preached what one might call a very simple faith, faith for the ordinary person. It seems that he himself was extremely glad that all the complications of Torah religion belonged to the past now that God made himself known so directly by an appeal to the heart, and was no longer accessible only to the religious. The disciples never forgot how he had once cried out in ecstasy: 'Thank you, Father, for your goodness in making your purpose known to these ordinary people. It is a surprise which until now you had kept hidden from the learned and the knowledgable.'

After Jesus' death, his disciples continued to follow his example. We have already seen what a powerful impact was made by this new faith in the cities around the eastern Mediterranean. Its success was certainly not least a consequence of its simplicity.

In the earliest days, there were no complicated theories, nor were there any sets of regulations which had to be learnt by heart. Anyone could become a member of a Jesus group, no matter whether they were an important official or a slave who could not read or write, a Jewish biblical scholar or a simple housewife. What kept members together was not any kind of special knowledge, but simple devotion to Jesus and his God, for whom no one was too insignificant or too vile. Knowing themselves to be loved, they discovered one another, and their mutual trust came as a surprise, bringing with it joy as a gift from God, the breath of his Spirit. There was nothing like an 'ordained ministry': the Spirit could make itself known to the group as easily through a stuttering slave as through a proselyte who knew the scriptures. Such a person might feel inclined to take the title of 'rabbi', teacher, specialist in knowledge about God. But in that case he was still firmly stuck in the old time. Now there was only one teacher, Christ, and everyone else had to learn from him; they were all his brothers and sisters.

Not much is left in our Christian churches of this original simplicity, much less the openness and mutual sharing. I was once invited to make a television series about Christ. In the second of eight programmes I sketched out the form of Judaism practised by the Pharisees in the time of Jesus. The Catholic with whom I was talking then suddenly departed from the script and interrupted me with some irritation: 'But what you've been saying about the Pharisees is precisely the Catholic faith as I have been taught it.' I was rather surprised, but not at the remark itself. I had to go through with the programme as the producer had arranged it, so all I could say was, 'I see what you mean, and I'll come back to the question in a later programme.'

Many people from what you might call good Catholic families were brought up on the notion that religion consisted of a great many obligations and a great many prohibitions. The enjoyable things were forbidden, and what you had to do was dull. And always there was the threat that sin might bring you to hell. Perhaps Protestants found things rather different, but rules were very important for them too: plenty of 'must', not much 'may' and lots of compulsion.

In all the churches there are constant disputes about the true faith. This is thought to be more important than anything else. There are professionals, theologians and scholars, who make pronouncements on the basis of their long study of its problems. These are the advisers to the authorities, to the Pope and the bishops in the Roman Catholic church, and to the synods in other churches. Many different churches each lead their separate existence, often in opposition to one another. Every church thinks that it has the truth and can offer 'salvation' to its members. This is very sad when one remembers what Jesus really wanted.

But a development in this direction was inevitable; that is the way human beings are made. Whenever we want to join together in doing something, to have a common aim or undertaking, we feel bound to make arrangements and set up rules. Even when we have some new sport, we set up an association, a club, choose a committee and make a constitution and a set of rules. These include the conditions on which members are enrolled and the regulations they must observe and the penalties for breaking them.

Every movement has to develop such a structure if it is to survive. The Jesus movement had to, and it had a very special reason for doing so. The new attitude to life which Jesus had preached and put into practice was focussed on the coming kingdom of God. Soon, he had said, God's rule would actually be visible, and that would change everything. He himself already felt its presence, and his followers should do so too; they were to act on it and live by it. However, this 'kingdom of God' did not seem to materialize. That was another reason why the Jesus movement had to get organized, and it did so very quickly. We know this from the earliest writings of the movement, the few letters which were certainly written by Paul himself, including the so-called 'First' Letter to the Christians in Corinth. Here we can see a Jesus group in search of an appropriate organization. The belief which had brought its members together was overwhelmingly new. What form was their common life to take? They had sent a letter containing a number of questions to Paul, who had introduced the story of Jesus to them a few years before and was now working with other Christians somewhere in Asia Minor. Moreover, Paul also had verbal reports about all the goings on in the Jesus group in Corinth. He had already written one letter to them earlier, but this has been lost. He wrote what is now called the First Letter to the Corinthians in about AD 55, from the city of Ephesus.

The letter deals with questions which were to be raised again and again in the future and which still concern us now. What is the essence of the faith that began with Jesus? How can we best express it in our particular situation? And what attitudes, what life-style does it require?

Many members of the group in the turbulent city of Corinth set great store by orators and philosophers. They argued about which preacher put the new faith over best, and which had the best credentials. Was it Paul? Or Peter? Or Apollos, who was an eloquent biblical scholar? Or is Christ himself the only preacher? Just what is the role of those who introduce others to the story of Jesus?

Sometimes there was such excitement at meetings of the group in Corinth that people were completely caught up in the new life, in utter ecstasy. Then they cried out: 'This is it, now we are risen from the dead. The time of rules and regulations has gone for ever. Now we can live wholly in the Spirit. No more obligations, we can do what we like!' But is this possible if you want to live as a group? Is it true that there is no future resurrection from the dead?

Meanwhile, they went on living as citizens in the great city just as before. If you were involved in a dispute and could not resolve it otherwise, you went to the law courts. It was the obvious thing to do. But once you became a member of the Jesus group, was it still right to thrash out your differences in front of the judge? Or there were questions to do with marriage: for example, did you carry on as before if your wife did not want to belong to the Jesus community? Again, if you bought meat in the market, it would certainly have come from the temples, which had developed into enormous slaughterhouses in ancient times. That meant it was meat from sacrifices, offered to one of the gods or goddesses. Were you still allowed to eat it?

Paul was a genius at offering answers and guidelines for all theoretical and practical questions. In each case, he began from the essential point, that those who had come to believe in Jesus were in a totally new situation. They had become 'a new creation', and all of them had experienced in a fragmentary way something of the perfect human life which had been realized in Jesus.

Paul's answers and guidelines were always very flexible,

adapted to the circumstances of the people to whom he addressed them. Later in the first century, we see in Christian writings a growing concern for correct, 'sound' Christian teaching, the desire to hold on to 'the tradition', the teaching of the apostles, in the midst of growing error. We also find increasingly detailed instructions about what individual Christians may and may not do, must do or must allow in a particular state or situation.

During the second century, the churches were very concerned about which of the numerous Christian writings in circulation were truly 'apostolic', written by one of the apostles or at least issued on their authority, thus giving a trustworthy account of their teaching. A canon, i.e. a list of holy books, was formed: our New Testament with its twenty-seven writings. Christians took over a Jewish way of looking at the Torah which had been developed some centuries before and applied it to the New Testament books: they had been breathed on, 'inspired', by God himself. In this way Christianity, too, acquired its holy book, a written record of revelation which could be studied by the professionals, scholars and theologians. With the text of the Bible in their hands, they could begin to argue with one another over what (and who) was orthodox or heretical.

However, although even in the third century Christianity still remained a movement, it was now firmly entrenched in some parts of the Roman empire. Still, Christians remained bitterly opposed to the 'ideology' of the Roman state. Roman citizens had to revere the state as a divine institution: the ruling emperor was to be regarded as a manifestation of the state god and to be given divine honours. Thus the Christian movement remained illegal, and some emperors used all the powers of the state in an attempt to destroy it, because of the threat it posed to their constitution. These attempts continued until the end of the third century, but they never proved successful. The movement had become too strong. Finally, in the year 313, Constantine legalized Christianity and made it an authorized religion; by the end of the same century it had even become the official religion of the Roman empire. The Christian emperors then used the powers of the state to persecute those who continued with the old religion.

This development is often seen as the 'fall' of Christianity. Before that time it was still a movement. I like to recall how in those days Christians were often thought to be ungodly, the atheists of their time. They did not go to church (i.e. to the temples), and they denied the existence of God (i.e. the official state gods). If you said to them, 'You claim to be religious, but where are your temples, your god and your sacrifices?' they would reply: 'The members of our group together form our temple, a temple of living stones! Our God is the crucified Jesus who lives and dwells among us through his Spirit; he animates our temple. We worship by sharing food and drink among ourselves, bread and wine in remembrance of Jesus.' This would seem incredible talk to anyone accustomed to the established religions, but when Christianity was transformed from being a threat to the state, into the official state religion, it lost all its strangeness. It began to conform to the old patterns. The impressive temples of earlier state gods now became Christian churches, solid buildings of marble and stone. The Christian temple was no longer an incomprehensible organism made up of a group of believers. A Christian liturgy developed in the temples, regulated to the last detail and administered by a hierarchy, i.e. a set of ordained, 'sacred' functionaries. There were official priests, as in the earlier temples. At the head of the hierarchical pyramid was the bishop of Rome, the capital, who was called the 'pope'. He was the visible representative of the real emperor in heaven, Christ, to whom all power in heaven and on earth had been given.

You can read in history books how the new form of Christianity developed further, and how it contributed to the formation of Europe. The important thing is what we are experiencing in our own time. According to many people, we have come to the end of organized Christianity. How has that happened? Whenever I am asked, I try to simplify a very complicated state of affairs by pointing to two particular themes: the stress on truth and the exercise of power.

The thought-patterns of the church which was established in the fourth century were Greek, and continued to be so down the

94

centuries. What I mean is that theologians asked questions about how things are in themselves, and how we can arrive at ideas and propositions which correspond as precisely as possible to reality. Many sciences still work in this way. In earlier times, it seems that people were unaware that the reality of faith lay on a deeper level than scientific realities, in the sphere of personal relationships and of the heart. So they would argue like this: Jesus is man, yet at the same time we worship him as God, even though he is not God himself; what, then, is the nature of his person, and how is it related to God? There was vigorous dispute among Christians over such questions from the fourth century onwards, and they often even led to blows.

If the authorities accepted a particular formulation as being correct, then it was made obligatory for everyone as an expression of the revealed truth. If necessary, both the pope and the emperor imposed it by force. As a representative of the heavenly Christ, the pope had control of all power. He delegated the worldly aspect of it, political power, to emperors and kings, reserving spiritual power for himself. He could hand over some of his spiritual power to bishops and lower officials in the hierarchy, and he could force the secular power to support him in the exercise of his spiritual power, often in order to maintain the true faith. At this point it is also important to remember that the Romans had long had a high regard for law and order. This helps us to understand the predominant place of church law and lawyers in the Roman organization of Christendom.

The result of this was an increasingly more complicated system of revealed truths, and a changing but ever increasing number of rules of conduct. In the sixteenth century, the Reformation seemed likely to revive the original simplicity and freshness of the early Jesus movement. But it, too, quickly gave rise to organized churches which also exercised spiritual power, though in a different way, and which also had endless disputes about the interpretation of the Bible and the true expression of Christian faith. In reaction to this, the Roman church came to lay more stress on the possession of revealed truth and to exercise its central power even more strongly. It did this in order to protect believers all over the world against heretical beliefs and misbehaviour, in other words against ideas and forms of conduct which deviated from the time-honoured old patterns.

Over the past century or more, however, the situation has altered almost out of all recognition. European civilization has changed with increasing speed, through continually more radical revolutions in more and more areas, including those of thought and conduct. Because the established churches had been oriented on traditional, centuries-old ideas of what was good, on the tradition of a divine truth and so-called Christian behaviour, they increasingly lost the support of those who had been involved in these great revolutions and therefore no longer felt at home in the old patterns. Many churches did their best to protect those who remained against the 'damaging influence of modern times', but they were not very successful. The Roman Catholic church seemed likely to do best here, thanks to the spiritual sanctions at its disposal. At the beginning of this century the church authorities utterly rejected 'modernism', which for them comprised any new ideas which Catholic thinkers and writers tried to reconcile with the essentials of the old faith. To give one example of their measures: every ordained priest, including those engaged in theological teaching, is compelled to take the 'anti-modernist oath'. This has become a formality, and priests are required to repeat it at intervals: I myself have had to take the oath three times in my life.

However, the strictest regulations have not been able to protect the members of the church from the new situation that is dawning. Consequently, tensions are increasing among those who try to remain members of the Roman Catholic church. I particularly want to mention Pope John in this context. There was amazement not only in the church, but also throughout the Western world and beyond, that the place at the head of that enormous power structure could suddenly be occupied by an ordinary and even honest man. Pope John brought to light something of what Jesus had meant in an astonishing way; and what he initiated, not least through his Vatican Council, had an effect throughout the church. Rome

96

cannot put the clock back now.

Rome remains unchanged in two points: its stress on the truth and the exercise of power. To oversimplify matters yet again, modern men have a different approach and take a different view. We can no longer summon up much interest in the question whether a statement about God and Jesus and the church and the Bible is 'true', i.e. precisely formulated and in literal agreement with age-old creeds. Our question about belief is not so much, 'Is it true?' as, 'What does it mean for us? Can it give meaning to our life? Does it give us a perspective? Does our communal life benefit from it?'

We now come to the subject of power. Since the French Revolution (to mention just one great event), the idea of some divine authority, i.e. that an emperor, king, governor, pope, has to be obeyed because he has received his power from God, has been on the wane. The disappearance of this idea has been accompanied by a growing sense of independence, the feeling that people who were hitherto 'subjects', not yet of age, have the right to make their own decisions. Nowadays we readily acknowledge the authority of others, but that is because of the persons they are, of their character and their knowledge, and not because they have been ordained and 'consecrated', so that a higher power can work through them and impose binding obligations on us.

There is a clear connection between the stress on truth and the exercise of power. Those of us who live in Holland can see this in the person of Bishop Gijsen, and his view of the nature of the church. According to him, the truths of the Catholic faith are far too difficult for the ordinary person, who is also unable to work out for himself how they are to be put into practice. The ordinary person needs an authority to guide him or her in the faith, the authority of Christ, given to the pope, who is represented by the man who has been appointed and consecrated bishop in Limburg. The bishop's helpers, the priests, have to be trained and taught in accordance with the guidelines laid down by Rome. Those who teach the priests are strictly supervised, and if they do not observe the demands of Rome, Bishop Gijsen brings the 'spiritual' power of the church to bear on them.

To many people, such an approach to church government seems mediaeval. It is obsolete, and certainly has no future. Bishop Gijsen may try to keep priests in complete isolation, so that they have no contact with 'modernist' ideas, but he cannot isolate his Catholic 'subjects', the laity, so easily. His own personal character and knowledge are inadequate for that, so it is to be expected that the group over which he still has control will continue to decline until all that is left is the bishop and his power-structure.

Is this one of the many signs that 'the end of organized Christianity in the churches' is at hand? No one can say. But we may be sure that the great revolutions of modern times have created all sorts of new opportunities, a climate in which Christianity can emerge in other forms and perhaps again become the kind of movement it was at the beginning.

The 'discovery' of the person of Jesus seems to me to be one of these opportunities. Discovery is the right word here. 'Historical' investigation of the Bible, including the gospels, only became possible in modern times, from about 1800. Before then, certain questions were never asked, e.g., How did the biblical texts come into being? What kind of people wrote them? What were they trying to say? What did they believe? What was their status in the society in which they lived? What kind of people were responsible for the gospels? They never occurred to people, because there was clearly no place for them in prevailing patterns of thought. Christians read the Bible on the basis of a particular set of beliefs, a closed system in which such questions could never arise. When the spirit of the time changed, and the questions were raised, the churches soon protested, and in this early period scholars who devoted their lives to giving answers were often excommunicated.

Thanks to historical research, 'discoveries' have been made about Jesus that were impossible earlier, including everything that we have discussed so far, his roots in Judaism and the way in which he came into conflict with it. The historical picture of Jesus and his purpose is a new element in Christianity. It seems attractive to many people and will doubtless have great influence. Let me single out two features of it. First, we now know that Jesus did not demand any recognition for himself: he deliberately directed people's attention to the love of his God for all men. In fact, he was even irritated because someone addressed him as 'good master'. Secondly, he simply summoned or invited people to make their own decisions, and never used any form of compulsion. As a result, we see more clearly than ever before how unlike him it was to argue endlessly whether he was God or God's son, and if so how, and how alien it was to his intention for people to enforce their views about such matters on others.

This does not mean that Christians of earlier times had the wrong ideas and acted in the wrong way. First, because we can now be sure that Jesus radically rejected this sort of assessment. 'Do not judge', he insisted. Here, too, he was utterly opposed to what was done by all the pious men of his time. His view was: the past is the past; all that matters now is that through your lives you should open up perspectives and opportunities for those closest to you; this is the only way of serving my God who has the future in his hands.

So when you reflect on Christianity down the ages, do not forget the good and the bad that are so intertwined in your own brief history. You could fill countless pages with a summary of the misdeeds and inhumanities that have been committed by church leaders and in the name of Christianity. But there is also material enough, if you are willing to consider it, for a demonstration of the way in which the basic substance of Christianity has never been forgotten. Hundreds of millions of people have believed in Christ and handed on their faith. They were of untold help to their neighbours and they lived and died in hope and expectation. No century has gone past without attempts from within the church to reform its structures in the spirit of Jesus.

'That's all very well,' you may say, 'but we are concerned with our own situation. The simple faith to which Jesus invited men should be creating new opportunities now. Given the crisis of organized Christianity in our time, surely another question arises. Can we have faith in Jesus and hand it on without any church organization?'

—=11=—

The Mystery of Jesus

'Why not Buddha or Mohammed?' This question sometimes comes up if I talk about Jesus with some enthusiasm. Occasionally other names are mentioned, like Gandhi or Martin Luther King. One feels a degree of resistance to praise of Jesus as a completely unique man. It seems to be one more form of the difficulty which so many people have over 'the pretensions of Christianity'. 'It is arrogant', they say, 'to suppose that Christianity is the only true religion. We can't take that. For example, such a claim fails to do justice to the countless followers of Buddha and Mohammed. Why should they not have their own way to "salvation"? If you make Jesus the only way to salvation, aren't you asking the whole of the Eastern world to acknowledge the superiority of the Western world in yet another respect?' And so they reject the Christian claim.

Can Christianity survive the rejection of its uniqueness? Is Christian belief conceivable without the conviction of its absolute truth, its validity for all men? Some people would say that this conviction is part of its very essence. A slogan from early Christianity ran: 'Outside the church there is no salvation.' We already find that belief expressed in the New Testament writings. There the church is compared to Noah's ark. All mankind (and all the animals) were drowned in the flood, except for those who had taken refuge in the great ship which Noah built. Similarly, you had to be in the church, to belong to the Christian community, if you were not to perish completely. Another New Testament expression means essentially the same thing: people are asked to join the church, because 'there is no other saviour than Jesus'. Behind all this lies the belief that every man is destined for eternity. He will be eternally blessed if he entrusts himself to Jesus, and eternally wretched if he does not.

The Fourth Gospel makes Jesus himself say this in a variety of ways, including the words that we have already quoted, 'I am the way, the truth and the life.' Of course this saying provokes the objection that Jesus seems to be self-important. I have tried to meet that by showing what he really said and did: how he pointed away from himself towards God and his fellow men, and how he served his disciples at table. Yet at the same time it is also clear that he was certain that the God of Israel was at work in him in an exceptional and decisive way; he knew that he himself was the instrument of God's last appeal to Israel, his last call for conversion. 'Whoever rejects me (or: my word), him will the Son of man reject at the judgment.' This claim remains the same no matter whom Jesus had in mind when he spoke of the Son of man; in any event his meaning was that a man's eternal destiny is determined by his attitude towards Jesus. That is quite something!

A number of similar claims were made in the Jewish world of the time. We have discovered that John the Baptist also saw himself in a decisive role; if people were not willing to be baptized by him in the Jordan, there was no chance of their surviving God's impending judgment. And to take a less well-known illustration from the same period, the founder of the Essenes, the group by the Dead Sea, saw himself in a similar light: anyone who resisted him was condemned by God, since it was through him and his wise interpretation of the Torah that God revealed his will. This 'Teacher of Righteousness' (his proper name does not appear in the writings which have been discovered so far) thus believed that he had been assigned a decisive role by God himself; he felt that he had been called, 'elected'.

The 'ordinary' Jewish faith of the time really made the same sort of claim: 'We have the Torah and that is decisive. Anyone who does not live in accordance with the Torah has no future with God.' It was 'the way, the truth and the life'. Outside the Torah there was no salvation, not for anyone. The other nations had no God and no future.

As we have seen, in the time of Jesus, this form of belief, with the Torah as God's definitive revelation to Israel, was still not very old. Much older was a belief in Israel's 'election'. That, too, was a tremendous claim, and difficult for us to take, with our modern views. We have become accustomed to the notion that all human beings have equal rights and equal opportunities, at least in theory. It does not occur to us that one people might be different from the rest, elevated above the others by special privileges, in this case a special bond with God.

How did the conviction of Israel's uniqueness arise? At that time every people and every nation had its own God. Israel saw its relationship with its own God as a 'covenant', i.e. something like a personal relationship in which each had obligations. Now that we know more about the ancient world in which Israel lived, we can see more clearly how exceptional this was.

When the people of Israel began to see their God in 'universal' terms, as God of all the world and of all men, they believed that their personal bond with him was the consequence of a decision on his part: he had chosen Israel for himself from among all peoples. However, the best Israelites never saw the covenant as a status symbol, something of which they could be proud. They sensed that God was at work in the world, and that his plan would only be fulfilled if it involved everyone. Israel had been 'elected' for a part in this plan. The people had so to speak been enrolled with the aim of making them the means by which all nations would come together in the recognition of the one God as their creator and king. The word 'election' should really always be translated, 'vocation to serve for the benefit of others'.

One of the writers of the first book of the Bible, Genesis, has expressed this conviction very well in the form of a story. He probably wrote in the time of Solomon, about a thousand years before Christ. He put together old sagas about the patriarchs and made them into a continuous narrative. At that time Abraham was regarded as the oldest patriarch, who carried his 'seed' Israel within him. To show what he believed about Israel's election, the writer prefaced his stories about Abraham with a series of narratives beginning at the creation of Adam, i.e. man, mankind. After that things went wrong. Adam fell out with God and one of his sons killed the other. Murder and vengeance increased, and then came the flood. Worst of all, as the writer shows in the story of the tower of Babel, mankind fell apart into numerous peoples who could no longer understand one another. Against the dark background of a divided mankind, which was really meant by God to be one family, he tells of the call of Abraham-Israel: in him all nations will be blessed.

This belief in Israel's task of serving mankind lived on down the following centuries in the hearts of one person or another, but it often faded into the background, particularly after the captivity, when the Jews needed to remind themselves of their identity as a group and to continue to preserve it. As we have seen, this led to the formation of the Torah. Their experience was dominated by a sense that they had been set apart as the only group in the world which knew and served the true God. They were the important ones, and all the other nations were outsiders. This was what God had willed.

However, the old sense of service on behalf of mankind continued as it were an underground existence. Sometimes one Jew or another expressed it openly, as in the story of Jonah. New expressions of the old faith came to be recorded in the prophetic books, which were becoming almost as authoritative as the Torah. Anyone who had a belief in God's concern for all men could find it in the holy books, whereas those who did not would either pass over the expressions of it or read something else into them. That tends to happen with holy books.

We have seen how this undercurrent of belief suddenly burst out with almost explosive power in the person of Jesus. Jesus believed that the God of Israel wrote no one off or, in positive terms, that the mystery denoted by the word 'God' is a love which goes out to everyone and seeks to embrace all men. He felt himself called, 'elected' to express this love and to make it a decisive factor in human relationships. That was what God had always intended. Israel had been chosen to carry out his plan and now Jesus was taking the task upon himself. He felt that he had been called to serve all mankind. If that seems pretentious, it was a special kind of pretentiousness, which did not make a man better than others but put him at their disposal.

While we are discussing Jesus' claim, I think that we should look more closely at the undercurrent of belief which suddenly burst out and came to life in him. We have already considered the prophets in connection with the appearance of John the Baptist. We can see how they expressed belief in Yahweh in a whole series of different ways, or rather, we can see how they experienced and emphasized certain aspects of that faith again and again. It is worth considering one or two of these aspects, which may perhaps make it clear how Jesus thought of his call, his 'election', and how his disciples understood it.

First, there is belief in Yahweh's faithfulness. About 750 BC, the prophet Hosea expressed it in an unforgettable way. He saw Yahweh, the divine partner in the covenant with Israel, as an unbelievably faithful husband. In our society a husband usually in the end gives up caring if his wife persistently runs after other lovers. Yahweh never gives up caring, however often Israel is unfaithful to him. He is God and not man, and he is always ready to begin again. This belief is expressed more or less clearly by other prophets, above all by the great man who lived at the time of the captivity and who wrote the main parts of chapters 40–55 of our book of Isaiah. This prophet believed in Yahweh as 'the first and the last'. On the one hand he is the ruler over world history: on the other he is the redeemer, the creator, the father and the husband of his people. He continues the same, even now, when there is nothing left of his people but the remnant from Judah.

Countless Jews over the following centuries lived by this faith. Many psalms express unlimited trust in Yahweh, who can and will save people from every disaster. Sometimes the writers suggest that he can even save people from the jaws of death. We saw how the writer of the book of Daniel expressed such a belief in the second century BC: God will give his persecuted believers a share in his kingdom, and will even bring to life those who have died.

Another theme is connected with belief in Yahweh as 'saviour'. He had manifested himself in this role at the exodus from Egypt. The people of Israel owed their existence to the intervention which saved them. But that meant that those who belonged to Israel had to become the saviours of others. To oppress a fellow man was to sin against Yahweh, whose nature it was to save from oppression. It was also to belie one's own nature as an Israelite, since the Israelites only existed because they themselves had been rescued. This had to be said extremely harshly when the people were organized into the two kingdoms of Israel and Judah. They were now divided into different classes and different social levels: rich who wanted to get even richer, at the cost of the poor whom they trapped and exploited more and more. The prophets attacked this evil state of affairs with great ferociousness. They were certain that Yahweh was on the side of the poor. This side of his character continued to be sensed very strongly as time went on. For example, prayers for a new leader of the people who would be 'a king after God's heart' seem to concentrate on the poor, the despised and the oppressed 'who have no helper'.

Most of the prophets also felt called to make clear to the inhabitants of Israel or Judah what it meant to be the people of Yahweh. They seldom consider people outside the two states. Their task did not lie there. It is, however, striking that they often talk about 'men', even when they are referring only to the people of Judah or Israel. To put it somewhat solemnly, 'they are universalists at heart'. What I mean is this: once you begin to talk in terms of a God who invites you, approaches you in terms of a person, as a human being, then your nationality no longer matters. You are a human being — everything else is secondary.

Finally, the prophets always came up against resistance, above all from the leading classes, kings, rich men and priests: 'I call you to be a prophet and therefore I shall make your forehead as hard as a diamond. Everyone will be against what you do, but do not be troubled. I am with you.' Some of the prophets described how they had experienced their 'call' in these terms. You did not have an easy life when Yahweh enlisted you in his service. It could break you, because your task was to proclaim, to reveal to people, the 'Holy One', who was utterly different.

Being the people we are we cannot accept such a God. So he can even have to reveal his nature through 'servants' who are broken by their work.

We can find a supreme expression of all these different attitudes, experiences and insights in the one person of Jesus. The faith of Hosea and so many after him, in a God who loves his people and will never write them off, determines the words and actions and indeed the whole personality of Jesus. Jesus' utter assurance seems to come from this sense of being loved by God. He even addressed God as Abba, which is quite extraordinary. Jewish children used the word as an affectionate way of addressing their fathers, rather as English children say 'daddy'. It would not have entered the head of any grown-up Jew to use the word when praying to the holy God of Israel. When a Jew said 'Father', 'my (or our) Father', in his prayers, he always added a phrase like '. . . and my (or our) king', to avoid being too familiar and to keep his distance.

Jesus himself wanted to communicate to his fellow men his perfect trust in the God who loved him. When God began to rule supreme, when his 'kingdom' became reality, love was to be the sphere of human relationships. Being 'converted' meant reacting to this now. Men were to live in an awareness that God loved them, that he had drawn a line under their past and had opened up a new future for them. It also meant that they were to treat their neighbours in the same way, always being concerned for others, keeping faith with them and not rejecting them, and always being ready to forgive, 'seventy times seven'. That meant the end of all attempts at self-assertion, complete detachment from one's possessions, including one's achievements and one's status. When Jesus' disciples told him that he was asking for the moon, that people would never give up what they had, he simply replied, 'For God nothing is impossible.'

The prophets preached that Israel's God was on the side of the poor and the oppressed. Jesus did more than just preach. He actually took the side of the 'sinners' in his society, those who were despised and rejected. In so doing he quite deliberately ran the risk of being rejected as a sinner himself, driven on by the

106

love of his God who would write no one off.

He always addressed himself only to Jews, to 'the lost sheep' of 'the house of Israel'. But we can see that he was also a universalist at heart. One has the impression that he preferred to speak about 'people' rather than about 'Jews'. Remember his famous saying about the sabbath. Only Jews observed it; the sabbath was an exclusively Jewish institution. It was regarded as a clear token of Israel's covenant with the Creator, who after working for six days was celebrating his eternal sabbath. He had given Israel the privilege of sharing in it as a sign of its election. However, Jesus does not say, 'the sabbath is for the Jew', but 'the sabbath is for man'.

The only name or title which he uses of himself seems to be 'Son of man', literally — in the Greek text of our gospels — 'the son of the man'. The expression is a puzzling one for us, as it was for Jesus' hearers. Perhaps some of them who knew the Bible well were reminded of the way in which one of the great prophets had always been addressed by God as 'son of man' (in Hebrew 'son of Adam'). That was Ezekiel, the man who was allowed to glimpse the glory of God. But in the language of the Jews, the phrase could also be used in place of the personal pronoun. Instead of 'I', they could also say, 'the son of man (or son of Adam) that I am'. Jesus talked like this. He warned a man who wanted to follow him: 'Do you know what you are asking? I am homeless. Foxes have holes, and birds have nests, but the Son of man has nowhere to lay his head.' In other words, 'I have nowhere to lay my head'.

At the same time, the term might also have a wider reference. In apocalyptic circles where books like Daniel were written and read, people sometimes spoke about a mysterious figure 'like a Son of man', whom they seemed to envisage as a kind of heavenly 'model', an ideal representative of mankind. Perhaps he was already in existence, but in any case he was to be 'revealed' in the future, and would control all human destiny. At all events, by applying the term Son of man to himself, Jesus could provoke a variety of understandings of the significance of what he said and did. Yet he did not give up his own personal secret.

Finally, many prophets were broken by their 'ministry', their task of making the voice of Yahweh audible to a rebellious people. We have seen that Jesus also came up against resistance and could expect a similar fate. In this respect, however, he went further than the prophets. His task was not only to make the voice of Yahweh heard, but to demonstrate the love of God in human form. Of course he did not see this as a special task, alongside or above his 'ordinary' humanity; it demanded his whole being. So, like the prophets, he was in the service of God, but in a way which consumed him body and soul, flesh and blood. He deliberately saw his work for the God who loves men as the service of humanity. He said as much, often, and also expressed it in an unforgettable way when he served his disciples at table and washed their feet. His last actions with the bread and the wine have the same significance.

Jesus completed his work by dying. Only thus could he become the supreme 'revelation' of his God. For when he had completed his work, died, and vanished from sight, he could appear to his disciples as a 'manifestation' of God. They began to see what they had only suspected while they were with him, as they were bowled over by his unprecedented air of authority and bewildered by the complete certainty with which he spoke and acted. Everything had once been mysterious and confusing, but after his death, when he had gone away, they began to 'see'. All the earlier Israelite experiences of contacts between God and man, divine revelation and the response to it by a variety of 'servants', now seemed to be realized in Jesus in an unimaginably simple and direct way. Jesus had expressed, explained and embodied Yahweh's appeal to Israel, his chosen people, and his search for a close relationship with his people; Jesus had devoted himself completely to God and had made a complete personal response.

In the earliest days of the church, Jesus' disciples began to express this belief in all kinds of ways, above all by telling stories about him. I think that their way of telling stories about Jesus caused a good deal of misunderstanding later on. Sometimes the disciples described their experiences with Jesus, what they had heard him say and seen him do. Anyone present could have corroborated such stories: we might say that the disciples gave an account of what there had been to see and to hear. Very often, however, their stories were coloured by their new perspective, their belief that God had been revealed in Jesus.

This sort of double approach is by no means unusual, as we know. You can consider people from two points of view. Broadly speaking, on the one hand you can look at them objectively, see them as others see them, or on the other you can make a subjective evaluation. You will not naturally think and speak about someone you love in the same terms as someone with whom you have a purely business relationship. And if you have to combine these two ways of looking at a person, you will realize just how different they are.

We have already seen how the Jews had begun to express their love for the Torah. It was in fact a book composed over a period of centuries and completed in the time of Ezra, about 400 BC. That was the historical reality; those were the facts. However, the Jews began to see the book as a 'revelation' of what the Creator had always willed and intended from the beginning. They then began to express a religious view of the Torah, i.e. their love for it, by narrating how God had made the Torah at creation before anything else. It had existed with God 'from the beginning'.

In order to express what they saw in Jesus, the disciples now began to do something of the same kind. What the Creator had really willed and intended from the beginning had now come to light in Jesus. So they *narrated* how he had been with God from the beginning, as God's express purpose, his 'Word'; indeed, Jesus had been present with the Father from eternity as the 'Son'.

At this point I should really give a large number of examples. Stories about the miracles which Jesus did during his lifetime are often much more an expression of belief, wonderment and love, a subjective evaluation of him, than a factual account from observers narrating what they saw and heard. The perspective of faith is dominant in the stories about the birth of Jesus. However, to go into this would take us too far. The important thing

109

for us to remember is that in later centuries people no longer felt that all kinds of stories about Jesus were told from the perspective of faith, as the views of devoted believers. In other words, it was forgotten that these stories were speaking the language of love. They were then seen as factual accounts, reports of events which anyone could have heard and seen, and in any case as descriptions of objective phenomena.

This gave rise to the notion that Jesus was 'someone' before he was born. He had been with the Father from eternity, so when the Father sent him to mankind, he was a figure who acted and spoke as a dual personality, both as Son of God and as man.

Another consequence of this notion was the idea of a 'plan of salvation'. For centuries, God had waited to send his Son, which in the fullness of time he finally did. Here too Christians have readily talked as though they were describing objective facts. This provokes mockery from others, especially now that we know that God's wait would not have been a mere forty centuries, as the biblical reckoning of time suggests, but many thousands of centuries. I was once sent an article from the German magazine *Twen* based on this thought: if God allowed mankind to muddle along for millions of years before sending his Son, why did he not wait a little longer, even two thousand more years? The time is now even 'fuller', with all our opportunities of reliable documentation and world-wide communication. Every event could have been recorded, from Jesus' first cries in the crib to his preaching, his miracles, his death and his resurrection. The message of the gospel could have been transmitted to the whole world, all mankind, by television. Countless problems for Christian faith would never have existed . . .

We deserve such mockery whenever we use the language of faith and love as though it were 'objective' language, language about facts. That makes us rather like the young man in love who asserts to everyone that his girl is *in fact* the loveliest and most beautiful girl in the world.

After his death, Jesus' disciples saw him as the most perfect man who ever lived, someone who had 'responded' totally to the mystery of God as it had been experienced in Israel, and who was therefore at the same time a reflection, an image, of God in our human world, his 'Son', who had made the 'Father' known once and for all.

That was their reaction to their experiences; it was their evaluation of that person and those facts. Jesus could also be evaluated in very different ways. The Jewish leaders saw him as a heretic and a danger to Jewish society. They reacted in this way on the basis of their beliefs. There are no objective reasons for disputing their viewpoint. One of the most penetrating scenes in Dennis Potter's famous television play *Son of Man* is the moment when the high priest is seen in prayer to God before the trial of Jesus. We should really have a picture of it in all the textbooks about Jesus.

To believe in Jesus means adopting the perspective of the first disciples and endorsing their evaluation, their vision of Jesus as the man in whom 'God' makes himself known. How we give content to that word 'God' depends in each case on our view of what really matters, the last and deepest questions of our existence, because this is what the word is reserved for in every language. Belief in Jesus, therefore, is something that affects our whole life and not just one more thing that we do.

But what does this imply, and how do we put it into words? The disciples had all kinds of words and images from their Jewish religion which they found very evocative. I have mentioned two of them, Word of God and Son of God; others were Messiah (in Greek, Christ), Servant of God, Saviour, Lamb of God, and there were many more. Moreover, the word 'God' denoted a reality which they did not doubt any more than those to whom they brought their message. The terms I have mentioned are now obsolete for many people, because they are virtually meaningless, and the same is also true of the word 'God'.

Modern men have to look for new ways of explaining why Jesus is the one who shows 'God' to us. Theologians, at least those who know what they should be doing, are still very preoccupied with this. I cannot remember who suggested that I might consider the following lines of thought. We ordinary people know 'from somewhere' that we exist and are alive, that we receive and acquire things which do not come from ourselves, but are derived as it were permanently from some other source. Yet we seldom if ever reflect on the fact. What is involved here is our existence, our life, our happiness. We try to keep it, hang on to it, as we must, because it is constantly threatened, and constantly weakened, by infirmity, misfortune, sickness, death. It is also threatened by others around us who try to get their own bit of happiness and hang on to it. In that case, we may come into conflict with them; everyone fights for himself, and in some cases the fight is a really hard one. Whenever we are defending ourselves, primaeval forces seem to come into play, which we experience as aggressiveness. At the same time, we know deep down inside that the fight is a hopeless one: for we are certain to die.

Yet there are moments in life when we feel very strongly that everything comes as a gift, as a present. Whenever we love and are loved, we share with others an atmosphere of trust and unselfishness. We no longer worry that we shall lose something; we give ourselves to others and in so doing discover ourselves. That is the way we feel. We cannot really express in words what we experience in love. But we know 'from somewhere' that we are close to the source of our being, to reality. Such love should encompass the whole of our lives, in that atmosphere of perfect trust.

This seems to have been the case with Jesus. He lived in an atmosphere of trust and extended it to the people around him; he 'created' the atmosphere for them. He seems always to have felt that his life had been given to him. He always appeared to be aware of its source, aware that he had received everything from his Father, 'Abba', the giver of all good things and the Creator. Jesus allowed this stream of Godhead to pass through him to all those around without any hindrance. He did not have to waste energy on securing what he had; everything was there to be handed on as a gift. He put the primal forces which ordinary mortals use in self-defence at the service of other people. He felt called to show them how they too could live from the source of their being, how they could give themselves to their fellow-men without concern or anxiety for their own affairs. Jesus seems to have been driven on, ultimately to his death, by that primaeval force, aggression, transforming into pure love what others use for their own defence.

This line of argument develops something written by John, one of the disciples from the earliest days, the author of the Fourth Gospel and the First Letter which bears his name: 'We have learned from Christ what love is; he has given his life for us. So we too have to give our lives for our brothers.' Only those who really help their fellow men in need know God and belong to him: 'Anyone who does not love, does not know God, for God is love.' You can recognize the followers of Jesus simply from their love of others, 'in deed and in truth', as the letter puts it.

The evangelist Matthew seems to go even further in his famous description of the last judgment. It is not necessary to have heard of Jesus to belong to him and so to gain eternal life. People live as God wants them to, and are near to him, when they forget their own concerns in order to help those in need: the hungry, those in prison, the homeless. Perhaps the description of the judgment goes back to Jesus himself. In any event, it is related to his story about the good Samaritan.

When I try to describe Jesus in these terms, as someone who did not assert himself, I sometimes hear a plaintive question, 'Does this mean that you think he was just an ordinary man?' My answer also takes the form of a question: 'What is an ordinary man?' I don't intend the question as a conversation stopper. Whenever I meet people on a deeper level than that of a fleeting acquaintance or a strictly professional discussion, I notice with constant amazement how each individual is really a world in himself, utterly unique and irreplaceable. At heart, each individual is a mystery which cannot be penetrated even by his or her closest friends and relations. I mentioned my neighbour's wife, aged twenty-nine. She has now died. According to the pastor who attended her, during her last days and hours she had a very strong sense of the mystery of her uniqueness. She was very much aware of the impossibility of communicating the ultimate. So, he said, she died at a moment when her husband was not with her; she wanted to be quite by herself.

Still, it has to be granted that when we talk about an

113

'ordinary person' we usually mean someone who has no exceptional gifts, achievements or influence. By that definition Jesus was not an ordinary man. He has gone down in history as one of the religious geniuses of mankind, and once we see him in these terms we have to recognize that he is inexplicable, a mystery. Whenever the ancient Greeks encountered someone who stood out above the rest, as an artist, statesman or sage, they said that a 'demon', a divine being, was at work in him. The Latin word for this was *genius*, a word that we also use in English.

The Jews who encountered Jesus recognized the same quality in him. 'A demon', a higher power, is at work in him, said those who did not know what to make of him. Think of the conversation about Beelzebub, the prince of the demons who were supposed to be at work in Jesus. The disciples came to recognize that the God of Israel had claimed this man, was at work in him and was 'revealed' through him. They were probably not fully aware of all the prophetic experiences and insights that I mentioned earlier. But they will certainly have remembered the old biblical stories about the way in which Israel's God appeared: to Moses in a burning bush which was not consumed, to his people in dark clouds with lightning and thunder, to others in blinding light. 'Anyone who has seen God must die.' Israelite believers were convinced of this because God is so utterly different. Yet God seeks to contact men, which is why he 'appears' so often, and says to people, 'Do not be afraid.'

This is the exceptional feature of Israelite belief. God is seen to be both far and near: wholly other, the incomprehensible and intangible mystery behind and in everything that exists, and at the same time 'someone' who seeks a relationship with people. Consequently that belief includes an insight into the mystery of human nature: we are made in such a way that we can be addressed by the wholly other, we are open to the infinite.

After Passover the disciples began to see in Jesus a manifestation of the God of Israel, the God who is distant and wholly other, yet who at the same time wants to be near us. Jesus was near to the disciples as the man with whom they had travelled round Palestine, with whom they had eaten and drunk and at whom they could look as they talked with him. At the same time he was utterly different, with that strange 'authority' that was so completely his own, with no obvious support, underived and incomprehensible. And what he looked for was also so utterly different, such a changed life-style and community from those we know, a reversal of all the usual standards. The 'kingdom' that preoccupied him, that was already at work in him and yet was still to come – another strange thing! – was indeed wholly other than what we might expect: it came from God, yet at the same time was a reality in the depths of our being. Jesus was a man who lived among us, yet at the same time he belonged to that utterly different world. In other words, he was a man who had responded completely to the mystery of God as it had been believed in Israel down the centuries, and who invites us to do the same.

It is fortunate that John sums up all these difficult ideas in the word 'love'. Love is something that everyone knows about, something that we can all experience, while remaining aware that this love which touches the very roots of our existence, makes us truly human, can never be reduced to mere words, can never be expressed completely and certainly cannot be explained. That is why when I try to describe it, I find myself at a loss for words. However, perhaps what I try to say will help someone or other to see clearly what belief in Jesus involves. His summons and invitation is to a way of life, a pattern of action, based on profound trust. Belief in him means accepting this, following as it were in his footsteps, seeing that the mystery of our origin, which gives us life and everything else, is good and not evil. It means being able to address this mystery, as Jesus did, with the word 'Abba'. Jesus shows us that we need no longer be anxious about that bit of ourselves that we call our 'own'. We are to share it out, give it away, let people take it from us, and then we shall find ourselves in the stream of divinity which we call God; like Jesus, we will finally be found in him.

There is no proof of all this. But if we begin to live in this way, utterly dependent on Jesus, in company with others who have the same concern, we shall become certain that things have to be like this, that this is the only way to a complete human life, to 'fulfilment'. Then we shall want everyone to discover the same way. Some people do not even leave things at that; they devote their whole lives to making their belief known and communicating it to others. This is their 'ministry', their way of following Jesus.

In objective terms, that implies that they too are making a claim: they have something that they want to pass on to others who do not yet have it. It is, as it were, their 'true faith'. But when they really live in the Spirit of Jesus, they are unlikely to seem pretentious, because they will treat others with respect, not obtruding and certainly not using compulsion, being prepared above all to be of service.

— 12 —

On Being the Church

More and more people are leaving the organized church to which their parents or grandparents belonged. They may want to live a good life, to be good people; some may even want explicitly to 'live by the gospel', but they no longer wish to be listed as members of a particular church.

Such people give all sorts of reasons. They lie between two extremes. On the one hand there are rather vague remarks like, 'I don't see anything in church any more', or, 'There's nothing in it for me'. At the other extreme there may be a well thought out rejection of any form of church organization, as being fundamentally in conflict with 'the Spirit'. Between the extremes a great variety of reasons are given: personal differences with ministers, indignation at some action by the church authorities which seems to violate ordinary human rights, or other objections and grievances of this kind.

I know a number of people who have no connection at all with the church, or who have now given it up. Some of them seldom, if ever, talk about Christian faith. Yet I count myself very privileged to be able to know them and to be with them. They do what Jesus invited us to do as though it were self-evident. Utterly devoted to their families, directly and genuinely concerned with the sufferings of others who may come their way, ready to help where they can — that is the way they live. It has nothing to do with Jesus or God, but they are not far away. I am reminded of the mediaeval saying *Ubi amor ibi Deus*, where love is, there is God. But I know better than to speak it out aloud. Nor am I ever tempted to use the expression 'anonymous Christians', which people who choose to be outside the

117

church can find very offensive: 'So they want to make us members of their club!'

There has been another development in recent years alongside the increasing alienation of those who were once church members. In many countries, including Holland, people have been gathering in small groups, as it were in 'mini-churches'. These have grown so quickly and take so many different forms that it is impossible to describe them briefly. However, their concern is always a practical one, to live by Jesus' invitation and example, 'by the spirit of the gospel' (or in whatever other words the thought may be expressed). It is also clear that the members of all these groups have more or less detached themselves from the larger church organizations; they may even come from a background where the church has long ceased to have any influence. We are not, therefore, talking about 'separated churches', like those found in some Protestant countries, made up of people who have found their church too lax or unsound in its teaching.

This development might be seen as a work of 'the Spirit', or rather, of the power which goes out from Jesus to teach men to live in love and hope. Of course he can inspire individual believers in the same way, for example, by means of particular texts from the gospels, and so on, but inspiration seems to be much fuller when individuals combine to form a group.

When we investigated how the 'church' came into being, we saw what the people in the first communities centred on Jesus found so astonishing: they came closer to one another despite all their differences, Jew and non-Jew (Gentile), Greek and non-Greek (barbarian), rich and poor, man and woman. The deep-seated differences which kept men apart, the impassable barriers between them, simply fell away now that Jesus had addressed them personally at the deepest level. Now the Jew no longer despised the Gentile nor the Greek the barbarian; they had been brought together. Similarly, the Gentile now recognized the Jew and the slave his master, as fellow human beings. Jesus was concerned to bring people together to form a community. One might say that isolated believers miss the essential element of faith in Jesus. Perhaps the figure of Jesus may awaken religious feelings or prompt vague resolutions in such a person, but Jesus himself was not concerned with that. His call was clear and precise, showing that people needed their neighbours. Those who share his faith with others, in groups, have more chance of understanding what his words mean and acting on them.

Furthermore, those who join a group find their personal thoughts and beliefs as it were shaken, upset, transformed, and at the same time enriched and deepened. They discover the experiences of others and are strengthened by them. They keep developing. What Jesus called 'conversion' also implied a constant readiness for change. To remain where we are, with fixed ideas and immovable points of view, is always an impediment to the love to which we are called.

From earliest times, groups of those who believe in Jesus have been called 'churches'. The word is a corruption, through other languages, of the Greek *kuriak(on)*, 'something that belongs to the *kurios*, the Lord'. We ought to keep discussing what being the church might involve in our time: how are we to form a community of people who are 'of the Lord', a community where he sets the mood? One can hardly say, 'Where he is the boss', because that name would not really please him.

From the very beginning, meetings culminated in 'the Lord's supper', a common remembrance, 'celebration', of what Jesus did on the last night before he died. His actions are unforgettable in their simplicity, summing up his life and work which, as we have seen, inevitably led to his death. It seems inconceivable that through these actions he still continues to carry on what he wanted to achieve: that by sharing bread and by drinking out of the same cup people can recognize his presence and learn to accept one another. Yet by receiving what he offers, we constantly experience that real life consists in giving. However, there is much beyond our understanding, and no one will ever be able to put into words everything that such an encounter means to them.

The Fourth Evangelist, John, has a description of Jesus' last meal with his disciples, but he says nothing about the sharing of bread and wine, the 'institution' of the eucharist. Instead, he describes another action, which he introduces in a very solemn way. Jesus knew that he had to depart from this world, and he gave his friends a supreme demonstration of his love. Conscious that he had come from God and was returning to God (as John puts it), he picked up a towel and a basin of water, and began to wash his disciples' feet. That was the work of a slave. When he had finished, he said, 'Do this for one another in remembrance of me.' What serving one another in this way means can be seen from other commands given by Jesus: 'Help one another, forgive, be generous, do not judge, be honest and faithful,' and so on.

To be able to live among people who are always aware of this is like being at a feast. So Jesus thought. He was fond of describing the kingdom of God as a feast. The kingdom comes into view when we find our way, in our time, of celebrating that feast and joining in it. I read somewhere what the Good Samaritan should have done in the twentieth century: he should not only have looked after the wounded man, but also have taken active steps to make sure that the road from Jerusalem to Jericho was safer. One could develop this idea further: in former times he would have wiped out the robbers or captured them, but now he would take steps to see that no one had any cause to rob others in order to supply his own needs.

We now realize more clearly than ever before that a good deal of misery and evil is the result of inadequate 'structures'. These can only be improved by political means. So belief in Jesus and membership of his 'church' involves political action. Anyone who ignores that fact lets the robbers have their way on the road to Jericho.

At the same time, however, the 'church' is a sphere in which we can also see that political action, even when it is inspired by Christianity, is only part of the story. The 'authorities' which need to be removed from power are also people who need relationships with others if they are to become fellow men. The leaders of a revolution can easily prove to be oppressors in their turn.

The 'church' ought to be an arsenal, or rather, an ever-flowing source of humanity. It can help by avoiding absolutes, and refraining from forcing home its views 'with all its might'.

We may well feel that death makes everything relative. The death of every individual and the death of mankind as a whole is a feature of our world. We cannot get away from it. In the time of Jesus, many Jews believed that God would make an end of this world because it was so evil. He would destroy the wicked world and make a new one, a 'new heaven and a new earth', in which he would reign supreme and would make men utterly happy. That is what their faith led them to expect. In our time, we too expect the destruction of the world, but not because we believe in God. We know *for certain* that the end will come. After many millions of years our earth began to have an atmosphere in which human life was possible, but this situation will not last for ever. Natural processes continue, and one day the earth will become uninhabitable of its own accord. We can speed up the process with our technologies, through pollution or atomic explosions, but we cannot delay it.

In the midst of hopeless situations, uncertainty, anxiety, guilt and despair, life can still be lived in love, trust and hope; there can still be belief in a future for everyone. Jesus can be the source of this life and faith. Such a hope defines the sphere, the area, 'the church', within which he rules and is recognized as Lord.

We can imagine what the church can and should be from what we know of Jesus. But we must communicate our imaginings here and now, in practical terms, to particular people. That is happening increasingly in the small groups which I mentioned earlier. In some groups the members share with one another whatever they own and earn, and live a completely communal life. They are full-time believers, like the monks of former times. Or there are married couples, for example, who also observe a particular rule of life. At the other extreme are groups which develop within particular parishes and communities. Here the members do not detach themselves completely from the organized church, but what goes on in its buildings and activities is on too large a scale for them; it is too much a matter of routine and too impersonal. They prefer to live out their faith in small groups, in which they can get to know one another and discover the nature of their call to

Christianity. Between the two extremes there are all kinds of other ways of being the 'church'.

I have often talked about this with young couples who have said that they want to get married 'in church'. Often they say quite spontaneously that they are not doing so out of any personal conviction of their own. The church does not mean anything to them any more, but their parents want them to be married there, so they are agreeing for the sake of their fathers and mothers.

When I begin to talk with them about what Jesus really wanted, what the 'church' ought to be, they often sound very surprised. 'But if that's what it is about . . .!' Their concerns for one another, and the way in which they want to begin their married life, are in fact one form of the church. So it makes sense to them to pledge faithfulness to one another in the context of Jesus' last actions with bread and wine. These actions were the sign of a love that remained faithful to the end.

A good marriage might be described as a mini-church. But married couples who want to continue to live by the inspiration of Jesus would also do better to join a larger group. Otherwise they remain isolated. What is needed is a group small enough for all the members to get to know one another personally, and for them to share in making an atmosphere in which Jesus sets the tone, where openness and trust prevail. Married couples can help others and also perhaps find in the group that third party in whom they may need to confide when something goes wrong, the third party to whom they can say things about each other which they cannot express face to face. Within such a group, too, children can be baptized as an explicit sign of a desire that they should grow up in the sphere of Jesus.

Perhaps there is a flourishing group of this kind in the parish or community where you live. You may find your place in it and be involved in it. But you may also have to look around for such a group, or even begin one with a few other people whom you know. Why not?

Smaller groups may differ in size and composition, but they are always likely to be found on the periphery of the larger church communities, sometimes within them, often outside or with roots in them. Here above all 'the Spirit' seems to be at work, enabling people to be addressed by Jesus. It may be that movements like this will one day begin to influence the main-stream churches, those leaden, cumbersome institutions. That is a possibility, but no more. For the mainstream churches have always been obsessed with maintaining, securing and preserving their own existence. A famous rule from the fifth century stated that Christians should adhere to what has been believed everywhere, at all times, by everyone. This automatically rules out new developments. They go directly against the aim of the organization. They cannot be seen as anything but a threat. Hence the expectation one sometimes comes across, that the end of Christianity and its organized churches is in sight. People argue that our world has recently changed to such an extent, at an ever-increasing pace, that the old organizations, which are essentially conservative, have no chance of survival.

What are we to think of such a prospect? Is it a cause for fear or hope? As a Roman Catholic I could talk endlessly about the positive possibilities of our world-wide organization with all its ramifications. Just think of the countless religious, 'liberated' to devote their whole lives to the well-being of others. The church is an incalculable power for good. But it also has many of the trappings of power, like diplomacy and money. I could also talk (and complain) endlessly about the way in which the Roman Catholic church and other established churches often take the wrong side in struggles for human rights against oppressive régimes.

Perhaps the 'church' is really an impossible undertaking. Do not forget that for Jesus the end of this evil world was near because the kingdom of God was already dawning. God would reign supreme, with absolute authority, over a perfect society. 'Eternity' is another way of trying to describe the indescribable. That is why Jesus could be so disturbingly radical about every-day matters. We must be prepared to give up all we possess, all the human relationships in which we are involved – parents, family – and even our own lives, for the sake of the 'kingdom of God'.

Jesus made one of his most radical, indeed anti-social comments to a man who wanted to go with him to proclaim the coming 'kingdom of God', but who first wanted to bury his father. In Jewish society of the time, burying the dead was a duty which no one was to avoid in any circumstances; it had priority even over regulations in the Torah. Burying one's own father was most important of all. However, what Jesus says is: 'Let the dead bury their dead. Leave it to them. People who still find funerals important now that God is almost here are not really alive. They are dead. You are really alive only if, like me, you have eyes for God alone.'

The first Christians also looked for 'the end', the consummation that was to be realized in a very short time. It no longer made sense to have a family or to start a business, much less to take steps to improve society. All this presupposed that time was going to continue, and it was coming to an end. The consummation, eternity, 'God' was at hand.

Even now there are many people, in both Europe and America, who imitate the first Christians and live in the expectation of an imminent end to the world. Sometimes they live in a permanent state of enthusiasm, and sometimes they adopt a radical lifestyle. However, they seem to me to be both unrealistic and antisocial. They do not want to take any steps towards the improvement of social structures and therefore keep out of politics. Because the world is coming to an end, they simply write it off.

That is surely the wrong attitude. We all need to live by the inspiration of Jesus, forming our groups but not getting into a rut. That is where the problem lies. Once we form a group we have to organize it, make rules, put into words what brings us together. We need to see and experience what distinguishes our group from other groups and from those who do not belong to it. Then we get involved in questions of true doctrine and proper conduct, in asking what marks out a church from the world around. Things cannot be otherwise. We need stability. We cannot leave everything to the ebb and flow of love. We also need to know what we are doing so that we can teach our children, and it is impossible to communicate what cannot be formulated and written down.

Nevertheless, we must try to make our groups more open, to

form an open church. We must try to live out our faith in Jesus together, but always flexibly, ready to give up unsatisfactory routines and forms and formulations. At the same time, though, we must never reach the point that our children no longer know where they are and our parents have no place where they can be at home.

Translator's Note

As Fr Grollenberg explains in his *Apology*, this book was written as a conversational book, closely following the style of the spoken word. Because of this there are no precise references to biblical texts, no chapter and verse numbers in brackets. Readers will not find it difficult to trace back the direct references to the original biblical context without such help. They may, however, like to know the source of the two passages from modern books quoted in the text. The quotation on p.6 comes from Isaac Deutscher, *The Non-Jewish Jew*, Oxford University Press 1968, p.21, and the quotation on p.77 from E. R. Dodds, *Pagan and Christian in an Age of Anxiety*, Cambridge University Press 1965, pp.137f.

Fr Grollenberg could not have been more helpful in looking over the translation and clarifying some difficult points; Sarah Hillard, Priscilla Hobson and Margaret Lydamore, with incidental comments from Linda Foster and Susan Molyneux, demonstrated that men left to themselves cannot be trusted to get everything right.

JSB